CALIFORNIA
NATIONAL PARKS

By the Editors of Sunset Books and Sunset Magazine

Lane Books · Menlo Park, California

PHOTOGRAPHERS

ANSEL ADAMS: pages 8, 23, 32. WILLIAM APLIN: page 61 (top). RAY ATKESON: page 51 (right). GEORGE BALLIS: page 31. ERNEST BRAUN: pages 61 (bottom), 79 (left). CLYDE CHILDRESS: page 17 (left). GLENN M. CHRISTIANSEN: pages 71 (left), 72, 73. FRANCES COLEBERD: pages 18, 19. KENNETH COOPERRIDER: page 20. ROBERT H. COX: page 75. RICHARD DAWSON: page 47. R. FISCHER: page 51 (left). CORNELIA FOGLE: page 14. FORREST JACKSON: page 7. SAMSON B. KNOLL: page 21. EILIF KUHNLE: page 22. MARTIN LITTON: pages 11, 17 (right), 24, 27, 30, 36, 39, 41, 42 (left; right), 43, 55 (top, bottom), 56, 57, 58 (top, bottom right), 59, 67 (right). ELLS MARUGG: pages 38, 45 (bottom). ROBERT N. MCINTYRE: page 69. PROCTOR MELLQUIST: page 62. DAVID MUENCH: cover. JOSEF MUENCH: page 71 (right). NATIONAL PARK SERVICE: pages 12, 13, 15, 40, 53, 60, 63, 67 (left), 68, 74, 76, 77, 79 (right). THEODORE OSMUNDSON: page 49. CLAY E. PETERS: page 50. JOHN ROBINSON: pages 45 (top), 52, 58 (bottom left). MARTHA ROSMAN: page 6. CLYDE SUNDERLAND: page 35. THE JAYS: page 22. U.S. FOREST SERVICE: page 48. JOHN F. WAGGAMAN: page 70. R. WENKAM: page 37. J. WILLIAMSON: pages 5, 28. CEDRIC WRIGHT: page 33.

MAPS by James M. Cutter, Deborah Neve, and Doris Marsh.

COVER PHOTOGRAPH of Vernal Fall, Yosemite National Park, by David Muench.

Fourth Printing August 1971

CONTENTS

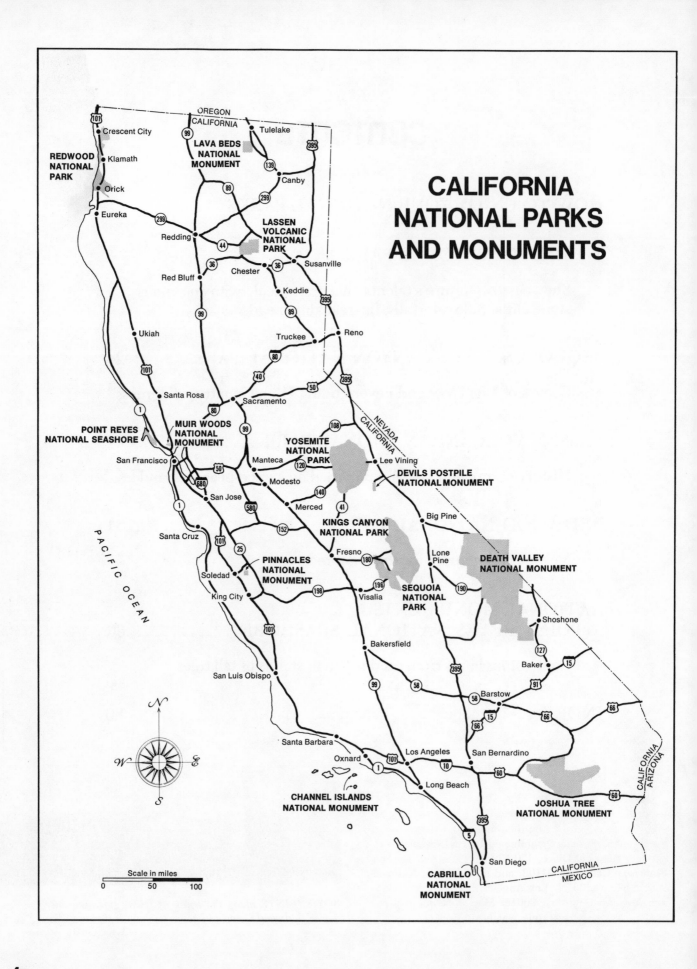

CALIFORNIA
NATIONAL PARKS
AND MONUMENTS

HOW TO ENJOY YOUR NATIONAL PARKS

California is fortunate. It contains more national parks within its boundaries than any other state, including the second and third oldest and the most recent park as well. Sequoia and Yosemite national parks were established shortly after the first one in the system, Yellowstone. Redwood National Park was established just before this book went to press late in 1968. There are also eight national monuments, the West's first national seashore, and many state parks and other natural and historical preserves in California.

The natural beauties and phenomena of this beautiful state range from the salt desert of Death Valley, to the tide pools of Channel Islands, to the rugged mountain country of Kings Canyon, to the redwood forest of Muir Woods. With such areas protected, it is assured that some of California's virgin forests will be spared, some of her waterfalls will never be harnessed for power, some of her mountains will never be desecrated by mine shafts and slag dumps, and some of her historical treasures will not be destroyed by vandals. The administration of these areas works to retain their natural value.

Each of the preserves has its own reasons for existence, its own value for the American people. Take advantage of these special offerings, plan to do things that you cannot do at home. This is what a "national park experience" is all about. There are opportunities to fish and ride horses, to camp and climb mountains—to explore nature and history close up and get back to your roots.

GENERAL INFORMATION

Too often visitors return from a national park to discover that they missed much that was worthwhile. Or they arrive in the park not knowing what it has to offer and spend valuable time learning what to see instead of seeing it. All of which adds up to the value of planning a trip to get the most out of it. This book will help you do that. In addition you can write to park superintendents for free literature on their areas, and visit or write the information offices maintained by the National Park Service: Regional Office, 450 Golden Gate Avenue, San Francisco, California 94102; and a field office, National Park Service, 300 N. Los Angeles Street, Room 2202, Los Angeles, California 90012. Map out your trip according to how much time you have; and once in the park, go to the visitor center for additional information or assistance. Also learn about the area from the many free programs it has—talks, museums, guided trips afield.

WHEN TO GO. More and more people are discovering the advantages of going to the more popular parks before and after the main summer season (about July 1 to Labor Day). Accommodations are less crowded, the weather is usually delightful, and most mid-summer activities are still available. Make reservations for lodging early no matter when you go. Write to the park concessioner.

WHAT TO WEAR. Too often ruined shoes (and feet) and chilly arms result when inexperienced outdoorsmen come unprepared for walking and hiking and cool evenings. Sport clothes are the rule, and most women wear slacks or shorts in the park. A dress is good for hotel dining, and a wrap and warm nightwear are necessities. On the other hand, summer days can be hot, especially

BOY SPRINTS along the trunk of fallen giant sequoia tree in Redwood Canyon of Kings Canyon National Park.

in Yosemite Valley and Cedar Grove in Kings Canyon, so be prepared for the two extremes. Know the climate of the area you are visiting.

ENTRANCE FEES. Most national parks and monuments have entrance fees, contributions that help support a fund to conserve our recreation lands and waters. They admit your vehicle, including trailer, and all your passengers, and usually cost $1.00 for a one-day single area permit.

The Golden Eagle Passport, the $7.00 annual permit to all the designated Federal recreation areas throughout the nation, will be sold for the last time in 1969. It can be purchased at most entrance stations, the American Automobile Association, and offices of various government agencies.

The entrance fees and the Golden Eagle Passport do not cover special user fees or service charges, such as rentals, boat launching, and sometimes camping.

FISHING. There is good fishing within most of the national parks, and it ranges from off-the-coast casting to lake and stream angling. Learn about the specific catch, best areas, and seasons from the place you are visiting. The required California fishing license, seasonal or daily, can be purchased at most stores in and near the parks.

SELF-GUIDING NATURE TRAILS like this one to Sulphur Works in Lassen take you to parks' attractions.

SOME REGULATIONS. Most rules to protect the natural beauty of the parks are well known—be careful with fire; don't be a litterbug; don't disturb the plant life or deface the natural features; don't feed or molest the animals.

Pets must be kept on leash or under physical restraint at all times in the parks. It is better to leave them home, for they will give you added responsibility and not have a good time themselves.

ADDRESSES. Individual national park superintendents may be reached for information through the following addresses.

Superintendent of Yosemite National Park: Yosemite National Park, California 95389.

Superintendent of Sequoia and Kings Canyon National Parks: Three Rivers, California 93271.

Superintendent of Lassen Volcanic National Park: Mineral, California 96063.

Superintendent of Redwood National Park: 501 H Street, Drawer N. Crescent City, California 95531.

CAMPING

The campfire, its smoky smell and crackling sound and its flickering sparks floating up in the dark; the smell of cooking camp food; the soft sound of falling pine cones and the crunch of pine needles and twigs underfoot; the lull of a creek running over rocks as you go to sleep, and the brisk feeling of early morning out of doors—these things are why thousands of national park visitors each year are campers.

If you are camping in the developed campgrounds, arrive early in the day to acquire a site. Also, don't neglect the more sparsely populated campgrounds out of the main visitor areas.

Campers and trailers can be accommodated in most park campgrounds, but full utility connections are rarely available.

PLANNING A HIGH COUNTRY VACATION

For the ever-increasing number of those who wish to get away from the paved roads and hit the trails into the back country, the California national parks, particularly Yosemite, Sequoia, and Kings Canyon, provide ample opportunity. Such wilderness trips take advance planning and preparation and an idea of what the experience will hold for you.

First of all there are backpackers, who go where they please unhampered by horses or mules, and are restricted least by cost. Generally, they carry packs weighing from 30 to 50 pounds (less for a woman). This type of back country travel tests your ingenuity in making one piece of equipment serve many purposes and in selecting items that weigh the least such as dehydrated foods.

SPRING HORSEBACK RIDERS ford the Merced River on an early morning ride to explore the beautiful Yosemite Valley. Park features like North Dome here take on new perspective from this vantage.

The next most economical way is to walk and lead a burro that carries the load, enabling you to take along more equipment. But a burro must be cajoled occasionally when there is not a meeting of the minds.

You can also rent riding horses and pack stock, but unless you are an experienced packer and are willing to get up early to chase stock that has wandered away, this is not recommended for your first trip.

Another way, popular in Sequoia and Kings Canyon, particularly with family groups that like to "stay put," is known as "spotting in." Here you walk to a predetermined campsite where a packer meets you with all your equipment and supplies or you ride in with him. He leaves until a definite date, either to set you at another campsite or to take you back to your starting point.

Finally there is the deluxe method, which subjects you to a minimum of discomfort and physical exertion, shifting most responsibility to the guide. He handles the horses, the packing, the fire building; and naturally this is a relatively expensive vacation.

An excellent book with hints on all kinds of High Country travel is *Going Light with Backpack or Burro*, published by the Sierra Club, Mills Tower, San Francisco, California.

Clean your wilderness campsite before leaving. Burn empty cans to get rid of odors, then flatten them to make them easier to carry out. Drown your fire and leave your site in such a condition that the next party will want to stop there.

If you are packing in the wilderness without a guide, be sure to check your plans with the superintendent or park ranger. Remember, once you leave the roads behind, you are on your own.

For planning and executing your trip, you shouldn't be without a topographic map of the area. These are available from the United States Geological Survey. Also helpful is *Starr's Guide to the John Muir Trail and the High Sierra Region*, published by the Sierra Club and containing routes, mileages, and kinds of trails for the area. It includes Yosemite, Sequoia, and Kings Canyon national parks.

YOSEMITE NATIONAL PARK

Showcase of nature's talents on a grand scale with enormous stone cliffs, tall waterfalls, far-reaching meadows

WORLD FAMOUS YOSEMITE VALLEY *displays its familiar landmarks. El Capitan rises at left; Cloud's Rest and Half Dome appear in distance; Cathedral Rocks and Bridalveil Fall are at right.*

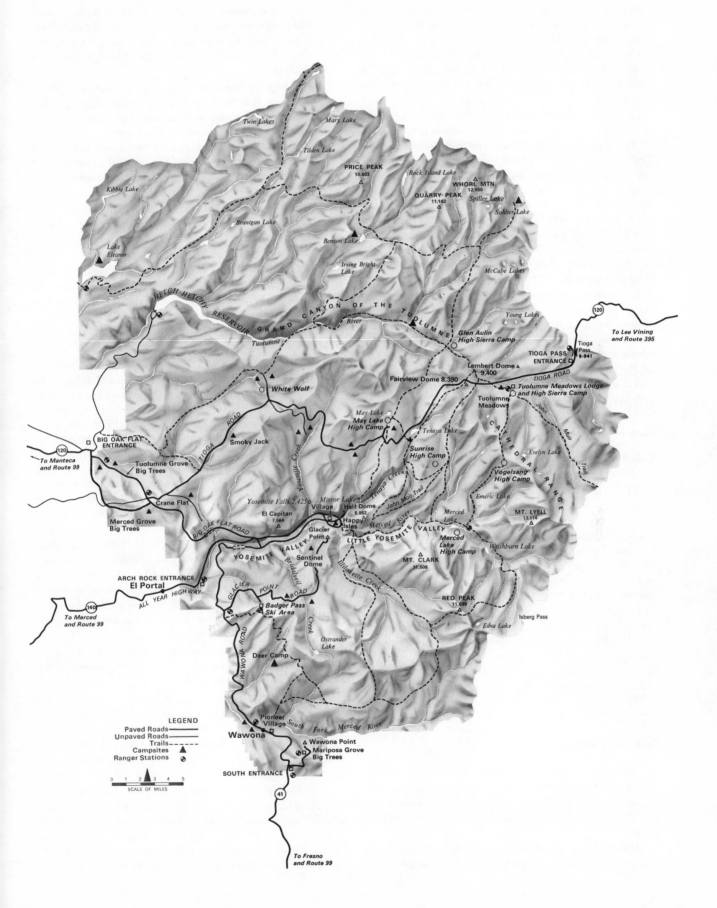

Twin Lakes

Mary Lake

Tilden Lake

Kibbie Lake

PRICE PEAK
10,603

Rock Island Lake

WHORL MTN.
12,050

QUARRY PEAK
11,162

Spiller Lake

Soldier Lake

Branigan Lake

Benson Lake

Irving Bright Lake

McCabe Lakes

Lake Eleanor

HETCH HETCHY RESERVOIR

GRAND CANYON OF THE TUOLUMNE

Young Lakes

120

To Lee Vining and Route 395

Tuolumne River

Glen Aulin High Sierra Camp

Tioga Pass
9,941

TIOGA PASS ENTRANCE

Lembert Dome
9,400

TIOGA ROAD

Fairview Dome 8,390

Tuolumne Meadows Lodge and High Sierra Camp

White Wolf

Tuolumne Meadows

May Lake

May Lake High Camp

Tenaya Lake

CATHEDRAL RANGE

Smoky Jack

Sunrise High Camp

Evelyn Lake

John Muir Trail

BIG OAK FLAT ENTRANCE

120

To Manteca and Route 99

Tuolumne Grove Big Trees

Vogelsang High Camp

Emeric Lake

MT. LYELL
13,114

Crane Flat

Yosemite Falls 2,425

Mirror Lake

Village

Half Dome
8,952

Merced River

Merced Lake

Washburn Lake

Merced Grove Big Trees

El Capitan
7,564

Happy Isles

Glacier Point

LITTLE YOSEMITE VALLEY

Merced Lake High Camp

BIG OAK FLAT ROAD

YOSEMITE VALLEY

Sentinel Dome

MT. CLARK
11,506

ARCH ROCK ENTRANCE
El Portal

GLACIER POINT ROAD

Illilouette Creek

140

ALL YEAR HIGHWAY

Badger Pass Ski Area

RED PEAK
11,699

Isberg Pass

To Merced and Route 99

Bridalveil Creek

Edna Lake

Ostrander Lake

WAWONA ROAD

Deer Camp

LEGEND
Paved Roads
Unpaved Roads
Trails
Campsites
Ranger Stations

Pioneer Village

Wawona

South Fork Merced River

Wawona Point

Mariposa Grove Big Trees

SOUTH ENTRANCE

0 1 2 3 4 5
SCALE OF MILES

41

To Fresno and Route 99

YOSEMITE is one of the most beautiful national parks by any standard. There is beauty of form in the graceful domes and towering cliffs, there is beauty of motion in the spray of its plunging waterfalls, and there is beauty of color from the snow-white dogwoods bordering the Merced River to the purple glow on the canyon walls at sunset.

Only 7 of Yosemite's approximately 1,200 square miles are occupied by the famous valley—which is to say that all too few visitors really see Yosemite National Park. The valley is notably the park's greatest scenic attraction, with thundering record-high waterfalls, carved granite domes, and sheer walls, that rise 3,000 feet on either side. But there are other beauties and wonders in this great park—glaciers, giant sequoias, Alpine meadows, and 13,000-foot Sierra Nevada peaks. One should go to Yosemite with the knowledge that not all is concentrated in 7 square miles, even though many of the accommodations and most of the people are found there.

Yosemite is a very popular vacation area. It offers an exceptionally wide variety of things to do and accommodations. And it is open the year around, with each season displaying its own particular charm. There are advantages to visiting during the "off seasons," especially in May and early June and after Labor Day. You will find a different Yosemite then. The park is uncrowded and quiet, and nature seems at her best.

How to Get There

Yosemite is only 4 or 5 hours drive from the San Francisco Bay area and 300 miles from Los Angeles.

BY CAR: From the north, Interstate highways 5 and 580 are fast approach routes. Then reach the park via Manteca or Modesto on State 120, or via Merced on State 140. From Southern California you can take State 41 from Fresno, or enter from Lee Vining on the east side over Tioga Pass. Big Oak Flat Entrance (State 120) and Arch Rock Entrance (State 140) on the west, and the South Entrance (State 41) are open year around.

BY BUS, TRAIN, AND AIR: Greyhound and Continental Trailways buses and Santa Fe and Southern Pacific trains serve Fresno and Merced. The Yosemite Transportation System runs its buses from Merced to the park throughout the year, and from Fresno and Lake Tahoe during the summer season.

Merced is served by United Air Lines; and Fresno by United and Air West.

Where to Stay

In Yosemite you can find accommodations from luxurious resort hotels, to housekeeping cabins, to your own tent. To avoid the crowds of the valley, don't overlook the advantages of staying at White Wolf, Wawona, Glacier Point, or Tuolumne Meadows.

YOSEMITE VALLEY. The Ahwahnee is one of the famous luxury hotels in America, the most luxurious in any of the national parks. It offers dinner dancing, naturalist programs, swimming, and beautiful grounds with cottages. Open all year, except for a short time in December, it celebrates the famed Bracebridge Dinner at Christmas.

The popular Yosemite Lodge, with Yosemite Falls as a backdrop, is in walking distance of the village and has a variety of sleeping accommodations from attractive hotel-type rooms to canvas-walled cabins, some with housekeeping facilities. Rates for two range from about $6.00 to $20.00. The Lodge has musical entertainment and naturalist programs on the patio in summer and a swimming pool.

Camp Curry, rustic and informal, has cabins, tent cabins, and some hotel-type rooms. Rates compare with those at the Lodge. In summer there are programs in the outdoor amphitheater.

WAWONA. The Wawona Hotel is informal but keynotes gracious living. It has a dining room, swimming pool, tennis courts, and is near stables. Costs compare with those at Yosemite Lodge.

The small and cozy Big Trees Lodge is located in the Mariposa Grove of sequoias. Cost is about $6.50 per person. You might enjoy having lunch on the patio.

GLACIER POINT. The Glacier Point Hotel is a 50-year-old landmark on the great cliff jutting out far above Yosemite Valley. Adjoining it is the original inn, the Mountain House, which was built in 1878 and is the oldest building still in use in the park. In summer the beloved old Mountain House takes the overflow from the larger 70-room hotel. But it is the snug haven for all the winter guests, who have to ski, snowshoe, or ride a snow cat to reach it. In summer, rates are about $15.00 for two in the Hotel, $8.00 in the Mountain House.

TUOLUMNE MEADOWS. There are no luxurious lodges in this high country. Concrete-floored tent cabins and a central canvas-covered dining hall where everyone eats family style make up Tuolumne Meadows Lodge, a camp high in the Sierra near a rushing mountain stream. It is just off the Tioga Pass Road near the Tioga Pass entrance to the park, and prices for lodging and meals are very reasonable.

Reservations are advised for all lodgings. To make them, write Yosemite Park and Curry Co., Yosemite National Park, California 95389.

CAMPGROUNDS are distributed throughout the park. The valley camps are open from mid-May to mid-September; the outlying ones have a somewhat shorter season determined by snow conditions. House trailers are accommodated at most campgrounds, but there are no utility hookups except at a private camp at Wawona.

There are seven campgrounds in the valley with over a thousand campsites. Showers and a laundry are available, and Camps 7 and 14 have naturalist programs in the evening. The Housekeeping Camp in the valley offers furnished tent cabins and rents camping equipment (supply is limited). The well equipped campground at

MAJESTIC LANDMARK HALF DOME dominates the upper end of Yosemite Valley as it rises 4,800 feet above the valley floor. The Ahwahnee Hotel is nestled in the trees at the base of the cliffs.

Wawona stretches for some distance along the South Fork of the Merced River, only a mile from a store. At Glacier Point there is a small campground near the Point and a larger one 8 miles away at Bridalveil Creek, both along Glacier Point Road. You'll seldom have difficulty finding a campsite, and there is a naturalist program. One of the largest camps in the park is at Tuolumne Meadows, where showers, a general store, coffee shop, post office, gas station, and ranger station are near.

THE DISCOVERY

The beautiful Yosemite Valley was known to the Indians for centuries, but because of its remoteness and inaccessibility it was not discovered by white men until the Gold Rush attracted thousands of inquisitive miners to the nearby foothills. The first Americans known to have seen the valley were a couple of miners in 1849 who became lost while tracking a wounded bear. One of them, William Abrams, chronicled the event with a description of the beautiful valley.

Apparently the first white men to enter the valley were the Mariposa Battalion who came two years later in pursuit of marauding Indians. They failed to capture the Indians, but they discovered a valley that was to become world famous. Convinced of the importance of their discovery, they named it "Yosemite" for the Indians they had driven out. The Indians, led by a chief named Tenaya, called themselves "U-zu-ma-ti" (grizzly bear).

Word of the discovery was slow in spreading, but in 1855, James Hutchings, guided by two Indians, brought in the first group of "tourists." Hutchings was Yosemite's first publicity agent, for upon his return he began writing and publishing articles about its beauty. The valley soon became the objective of many who were of durable enough condition to make the strenuous trip. Many influential persons visited Yosemite, and the idea that the area should be set aside to protect it from exploitation soon gained momentum. In 1864, President Lincoln signed an act providing that the area of the valley and the Mariposa Grove of Big Trees be granted to California for "public use, resort, and recreation, unalienable for all time." In 1868, after his visit to what is now the park, John Muir immediately began to write about the area and to fight for its further preservation. Largely as a result of his efforts and those of publisher Robert Underwood Johnson, Congress was influenced to act again in Yosemite's behalf. In 1890, Yosemite National Park was established around the state grant made by Lincoln. So there was, in effect, a state park surrounded by a national park. In 1906, the state ceded the original grant

TALL YOSEMITE FALLS has three separate parts and a thundering roar when it is full volume in spring.

back to the Federal Government, thus ending a period of dual administration and setting up the park's area as we know it today. Yosemite's fascinating history is well told by exhibits in the Pioneer Village at Wawona.

NATURAL FEATURES

Yosemite's world-famous valley is undoubtedly the park's greatest single feature. Seven miles long, over a mile wide, with walls that rise more than 3,000 feet above the floor, the valley and the story of its formation is a lesson found in many geology textbooks. The Merced River rushes into the valley at the upper end after a tumultuous journey from its origin in the High Country.

It makes the long drop at Nevada Fall and another plunge at Vernal Fall a mile below, then winds through Yosemite Valley to join the San Joaquin River a hundred miles to the west.

The valley is composed of many individual natural attractions. The great waterfalls are among the highest and most spectacular in the world. Of these, Ribbon Fall has the greatest single drop—1,612 feet. The most famous is Yosemite Falls, which is made up of three parts, the Upper Fall, the cascades, and the Lower Fall. The three combined drop 2,425 feet from the rim. The upper fall alone is over eight times the height of Niagara. While more water rushes over Nevada and Vernal falls on the Merced River, Yosemite Falls seems to dominate because of its height and because in spring its thundering roar can be heard throughout the valley. If you are near enough, you feel the ground tremble with the terrific impact of falling tons of water. Other waterfalls in the valley known for their beauty and size are Bridalveil (620 feet), Nevada (594 feet), Vernal (317 feet), and Illilouette (370 feet).

The waterfalls are at their peak during May and June. Many visitors who come after that time are disappointed at not seeing them at their best or, in some cases, not seeing them at all. Nevada and Vernal falls of the Merced River are active all year. A few of the falls on the sides of the valley will run through the entire summer if the snow pack in the mountains is unusually heavy and snow melt is slow, but in ordinary years there is no evidence of them after mid-August.

The great granite domes are another natural feature of the park, and the largest ones are found in the valley. Half Dome is king, dominating the upper end of Yosemite Valley as it rises 4,800 feet above the floor and looks down upon its neighbors North Dome and Basket Dome. While not a dome, El Capitan raises its massive stone head 3,000 feet above the valley floor and seems to salute the visitor taking the unobstructed look from Valley View. El Capitan is a monolith, said to be the largest single block of granite in the world and much greater in volume than the Rock of Gibraltar. Sentinel Dome is near Glacier Point, and Lembert Dome is in Tuolumne Meadows.

The meadows of Yosemite are delightful, especially in spring when the ground is moist, growth is deep and luxurious, and wildflowers are most evident. There are several large lush meadows on the valley floor. In the country above the rim, Tuolumne Meadows are the most extensive and best known. Here flowers bloom in profusion, and a network of small streams keeps the meadows moist throughout the summer.

The High Country is definitely a characteristic and important feature of Yosemite. It is a land of rugged peaks, glistening mountain lakes, glaciers, polished granite, and spectacular domes—beauty undreamed of by the visitor who ventures no farther than the valley. This land easily rivals certain parts of Kings Canyon in grandeur, and is readily accessible; you can drive into the heart of it at Tuolumne Meadows. Yosemite's 700 miles of trails, including the well known High Sierra Loop, take you far inside this High Country—among the finest in the Sierra.

How It Came About

The visitor to Yosemite cannot help but wonder what formed the spectacular natural features that characterize Yosemite. To start the story somewhere, we will pick a time about 130 million years ago when the country now occupied by the Sierra Nevada was covered with a series of parallel ridges running in a general northwest-southwest direction. Under these ridges were the granites seen in Yosemite today.

Over millions of years water eroded the ridges and exposed the granites and produced a land of low rolling hills and broad valleys. Drainage was then to the southeast into a slow, sluggish stream later to become the Merced River.

At length, a great upheaval lifted and tilted a piece of the earth's crust so huge that it covered the entire area of what is now the Sierra Nevada. This great section, known as the Sierra Block, tilted so that on the east there was an escarpment rising from what is now Owens Valley where such towns as Bishop, Lone Pine, and Independence are located. On the west, the great block sloped gradually down to blend into what we now know as the Central Valley of California.

The streams which used to be sluggish were then given new life by the increased slope, and they raced toward the Pacific, cutting deep canyons. The ancestor of the Merced River was among the streams that took on new life, and it rushed seaward, carving a canyon 2,000 feet deep. The tributary streams feeding into it from the north and south continued on about the same gradient as before, because there was nothing to accelerate their flow, and the Merced left them behind. The deeper it cut, the higher the tributary streams were stranded above it. Thus were born the hanging valleys and the waterfalls of today.

But this was not yet the end, for the climate changed a million or more years ago, and ice began accumulating in the high country to a thickness of thousands of feet. In time, glaciers carrying abrasive sandstone and boulders frozen in the ice moved down the slopes, grinding and gouging as they progressed and giving the landscape a still different appearance. The V-shaped and stream-cut valleys were deepened and widened by the ice and became U-shaped. The terrific pressure—90 tons or more per square foot—rounded off great masses of granite forming domes like Fairview and Lembert, and in certain sections the weight planed and polished large areas of granite to mirror smoothness. Other domes were formed by an erosion process called exfoliation. For example, Sentinel Dome was probably rounded millions of years before the glacial ages and was never covered with ice.

At least three times the glaciers advanced and then receded, the last advance leaving a great pile of rock debris in the vicinity of El Capitan. This natural dam formed a lake 5½ miles long, which later gave the valley its flat floor.

The many holes gouged by the glaciers in their slow journey filled with water to become a thousand sparkling mountain lakes.

There are still glaciers in the Sierra, remnants of once mighty ice sheets. In Yosemite, Lyell Glacier can be reached by trail from Tuolumne Meadows, and is measured carefully each year by the National Park Service

EL CAPITAN, *the huge granite monolith, stands as a sentinel at the lower end of Yosemite Valley.*

TRACES OF THE ICE AGE

Dramatic evidences of the Ice Age in Yosemite make the events of the glacial epoch of 10,000 years ago seem less remote. The great power of the prehistoric glaciers left obvious marks on the land that you can spot as you travel through the park.

Glacial Polish. Among the largest expanses of the glossy granite rock are those visible in the upper canyon of Merced River. You see them from trails to Merced, Washburn, and Vogelsang lakes; the trail to Cloud's Rest; and the Sunrise Trail.

In the valley you can find glacial polish near Mirror Lake and at Rocky Point, about 25 feet above the base of the cliff. Glacial polish can also be seen along the Tioga Road, particularly in the Lake Tenaya area and in Tuolumne Meadows.

Moraines. A glacier deposits accumulated debris called moraine along its side and at its terminus. Along the south valley road near Bridalveil Fall, a road-cut across the Bridalveil Moraine reveals an unsorted pile of boulders and coarse and finely ground rock, called till, left as a ridge by a glacier. Contrast the boulder-strewn river here with the sandy bed upstream.

Along the north valley road east of Valley View, a ridge in the forest extending toward the river was left by the same glacier. You'll find another moraine up-river from Camp 12 near the valley stables.

Remnants of glacial deposits may be seen along the Tioga Road between Smoky Jack campground and the turnoff to May Lake. Others are east of Lembert Dome, and in Dana Meadows, south of the Tioga Pass park entrance. Roadside forests of red fir grow on many of these glacial till deposits.

Erratics. These large boulders were torn from distant mountains and left at their present sites when the ice melted. At Olmsted Point, west of Tenaya Lake on the Tioga Road, erratics trace the path left by the Tenaya Glacier. More erratics are east of Tenaya Lake.

Domes. Perhaps the park's most prominent examples of glaciation are its domes. Outstanding examples of glacier-carved domes are Fairview and Lembert and others in Tuolumne Meadows.

GLACIER-POLISHED granite near Mirror Lake, best example in Yosemite, glistens in early morning sun.

to record changes. Park naturalists and exhibits at the main visitor center in Yosemite Village also give accounts of the formation of this land.

Plants and Animals

The giant sequoias of Sequoia and Kings Canyon national parks are larger and more extensive, but Yosemite has "the tree you can drive through," the well known Wawona (tunnel) Tree in Mariposa Grove. Largest of the three sequoia groves in Yosemite, Mariposa Grove is a few miles inside the South Entrance.

The other two, the Tuolumne and Merced groves, are located near Crane Flat on the Big Oak Flat Road. A detailed section on giant sequoias is in the Sequoia and Kings Canyon chapter.

The flowers of Yosemite are characteristic of the Sierra, and they are profuse and varied. More than 1,200 species occur in the park. A botanist can have a field day in the extraordinary range (2,000 to over 13,000 feet) of elevation that includes five plant belts. There is a satisfying variety of flora, even along the road. Along the river in the valley, the Pacific dogwood and azalea are especially beautiful in the spring. Also found at this time, particularly in the shelter of the coniferous forests as the snow is receding, is the brilliant red snow plant.

Guided wildflower walks above the south rim of the valley are part of the park's naturalist program in July and August. There are easy 3-hour-or-so jaunts combining drives and walks between Badger Pass Ski Area and Bridalveil Creek Camp. The booklet *Wildflowers of the Sierra* (Yosemite Natural History Association), available in the park, is a helpful reference. Other more frequent walks are conducted during the summer. Dates are posted at main centers in the park.

In general, Yosemite is heavily forested. On the valley floor are big incense cedars, often mistaken for sequoias, and there are tall ponderosa or yellow pines. One of the most frequently encountered trees in the valley is California black oak with its small evergreen leaves. Higher up is the big Jeffrey pine looking much like the ponderosa. Here also grow firs and, still higher, the white-barked pine. One of the finest stands of sugar pine remaining in the world was presented to the park not too long ago by the Rockefeller interests to save it from being cut for lumber. It is located along Tuolumne Grove Auto Nature Trail which starts at Crane Flat.

You will probably see more large wildlife in Yosemite than in any other California park. Deer are often seen in the meadows and along the roads. It is difficult to believe that the gentle-appearing creatures can be dangerous, but each year many people are injured who do not heed the park's rules to leave the animals alone. Bears are seen along the roads and sometimes in the camps, where they like to upset the garbage. Bears are especially dangerous. There is a strict park regulation that prohibits feeding any of the animals.

Animals of the park are those common to the rest of the Sierra Nevada. About 75 different species of mammals and 220 kinds of birds make their homes in Yosemite.

YOSEMITE REGIONS

It is difficult to partition a park such as this into regions, but different sections do have their own special characteristics. For the sake of clarity and to familiarize you with various attractions in the park, we will designate different general areas.

The visitor center in the Village is an important stop early in your Yosemite visit. An educational introduction to the park from exhibits, rangers, and staff will help you plan your trip and select from the things mentioned here, if you cannot fit them all in.

The Valley

The legendary beauty of Yosemite Valley is a reality. Majestic granite cliffs rise abruptly from the level floor; white waterfalls surge and tumble noisily over walls of awesome height and flow through the forested valley as the Merced River and many active streams. Only one-half of one per cent of Yosemite's total area, it displays more than its share of the park's scenic beauty. Here, you'll see Half Dome, El Capitan, Cathedral Peaks, and Yosemite Falls. The valley has become the central visitor attraction of the park, and most of the recreational opportunities and accommodations are here, including the hospital, the major stores, and shops. A shuttle bus serves the valley all day long, and a sightseeing tramcar takes trips daily around the valley from Happy Isles in the east to Wawona Tunnel in the west.

If you choose to avoid crowds, you may want to headquarter elsewhere in the park and visit the valley on occasion. The other alternative is to visit in May or early June, or in September or October. Most of the facilities are operating (many are open all year), you will not find the crowds, it is not so hot, and the landscape is at its best.

SADDLE HORSE PARTY with guide approaches Nevada Fall while exploring magnificent Yosemite Valley.

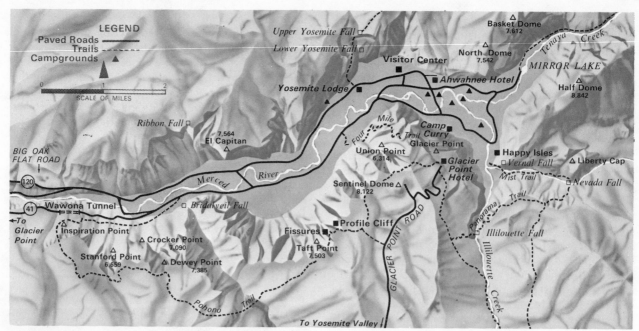

YOSEMITE VALLEY AND GLACIER POINT landmarks can be located with this map. Also note the three Yosemite trails, Four-Mile, Pohono, and Panorama, that are described later in this chapter.

Among the various things to do in the valley, trail-wandering is one of the most enjoyable. The trails are wide, usually shady, comparatively level, and lead to out-of-the-way places. There is one short walk of a quarter mile which you should take. Drive your car to the Yosemite Falls Parking Area and walk at least as far as the rustic bridge over Yosemite Creek. Some say the bridge is enchanted and that if you listen, you will hear voices in the stream. Enchanted or not, from this point you will get a much better idea of the terrific power and volume of Yosemite Falls. From Happy Isles you can take the worthwhile 1½-mile trip to the top of Vernal Fall, where you can lie on the smooth granite and watch water dropping 317 feet. If you are not tired, go on for another mile to the larger Nevada Fall. If you are looking for something more strenuous, climb the wall to Glacier Point over the Four-Mile Trail which starts near the base of Sentinel Rock.

Bicycling is a favorite sport here. It is a leisurely and enjoyable way to visit various points in the valley.

Horses can be rented at the Yosemite Stables, and while many prefer to take all-day trips to the rim, others use the cool shaded bridle paths which wind over the valley floor. The valley stables, largest of four within the park and the only one offering saddle horses for rent in the spring, opens for business on April 30, when early-season visitors have an opportunity to enjoy the valley at its uncrowded best.

Guided rides leave at 8 and 10 A.M. and at 1 and 3 P.M., and cost $3.50 per person for the 2-hour ride. Riders must be at least 7 years old. There is a pony ring for younger children. Donkeys which may be led outside the ring are also available.

Few national parks offer the extensive interpretive program that Yosemite does. There are two museums, the visitor center in Yosemite Village and the Nature Center at Happy Isles. You will enjoy the wildflower garden behind the visitor center and the Indian talks and basket-weaving demonstration given there daily. Ranger naturalists are there to interpret park features and satisfy the curiosity of visitors. Ask them questions any time.

The naturalist programs include all kinds of conducted trips. Campfire programs offered at several campgrounds have community singing; illustrated talks are featured at the Lodge and Camp Curry.

The Junior and Senior Ranger program is a nature school located at the Happy Isles Nature Center. Junior Rangers are in grades 3 through 6; Senior Rangers in grades 7 through 12. Classes meet every weekday to study Yosemite's animal life, rocks, trees, and flowers. A badge is given upon completion of the course, and boys and girls can take home the scrapbook they have made as a reminder of their Yosemite visit. There is a nominal fee for the school, about 25 cents per day, sufficient to pay for the materials used.

Happy Isles itself is delightful, especially in early morning and evening. Here the Merced River breaks up into fingers and flows around several tiny islands. It is an interesting place at any time of day, for it is a trail hub where you will see backpackers and horseback parties taking off and returning from the High Country.

Across from the visitor center is the little pioneer cemetery. The first two guardians of Yosemite after Lincoln granted it to California, Galen Clark and James Hutchings, are buried here, as are many of the old

BICYCLE TOUR of valley floor is pleasant and colorful in autumn. Sentinel Rock is towering backdrop.

COVERED BRIDGE at Wawona, built in 1858, looked like this before it was restored and strengthened.

Yosemite Indians. Some wooden markers state simply "Boy," "Lucy," and "Mother of Lucy."

Be sure to see all the falls and domes in the valley, and at the lower end just off the main road see the huge monolith El Capitan. Some early morning or evening, stand at the base of this great granite mass, look up and marvel.

Mirror Lake, where impressive Easter morning services are held, is a worthy attraction in the upper valley.

The Wawona Region

Known for its grove of giant sequoias, the Wawona region is near the South Entrance at about the same altitude as the valley (4,000 feet), and is a popular place to stay.

The outstanding feature of the Wawona region, the Mariposa Grove of giant sequoias, is the other part of President Lincoln's original grant for preservation. You may have heard about this grove because of its famous Wawona Tree, "the tree you can drive through." The tunnel was cut in 1881 to permit the passage of horse-drawn stagecoaches.

In the Mariposa Grove there are over 200 trees 10 feet or more in diameter and thousands of smaller ones. The largest tree in Yosemite, and probably the oldest one, is the Grizzly Giant which approaches the size of the largest tree in the world, the General Sherman of Sequoia National Park, with a height of 209 feet and a basal diameter of 34.7 feet. Wandering through the groves gives one a serene feeling and a reverent attitude for these long living giants of nature.

Under the great trees is a rustic log cabin as interesting in itself as the exhibits of the sequoias which it contains. The original cabin was built in 1885-86 by Galen Clark and used as a rest stop and place where "natural curiosities" were sold. By the 1920's, the cabin was in a bad state of repair, and a small museum duplicating the appearance of the original was built on the site. It is quite possible that before long the museum will be changed in location, for there is thought of moving it near the South Entrance. Talks are given at the cabin each day by ranger naturalists.

A little over 2 miles beyond the Big Trees museum at the termination of the road is Wawona Point. From here unfolds a beautiful panorama of the country below and beyond.

The respect for the great trees of this country was aptly communicated by California poet Edwin Markham.

"These mighty trees belong to the silences and the millenniums. Many of them have seen a hundred human generations rise, give off their little clamors, and perish. They chide our pettiness. They rebuke our impiety. They seem indeed to be forms of immortality standing here among the transitory shapes of time."

Near the Wawona Hotel is a picturesque covered bridge, originally built as an open structure by Galen Clark in 1858 and covered by the Washburn brothers in 1875. Over the years it was so weakened by age and periodic high water that it became unsafe and was in danger of being washed away. Realizing its unique quality and historical significance, the National Park Service has restored it recently, using as many of the original timbers as possible. It has become the nucleus

ROARING CASCADE of white water, Nevada Fall provides refreshing stop along the Panorama Trail.

of the Wawona Pioneer Village where there are exhibits, old stagecoaches, and authentic cabins and houses that tell the story of early Yosemite life.

Glacier Point

The view is the thing at Glacier Point—a tremendous sweep of the length of the valley in both directions. Half Dome is at your front door; Vernal Fall is prominent; and beyond rise the snow-clad peaks of Yosemite's back country. You look down into a world of miniature people, cars, and buildings, the largest being the doll-house-sized Ahwahnee Hotel. The Merced River is a tiny creek, and the roads are a network of dark ribbons. You will want to visit the Glacier Point Lookout not only to drink in the view but to study the exhibits in the semi-open structure a few hundred yards from the Glacier Point Hotel.

The old route to Glacier Point is a beautiful narrow road that winds its way through the forest and around lush meadows between the Badger Pass Ski Area and Bridalveil Creek Campground. There are few people who know about it, or at least who use it today, but it is a charming little road and part of that charm lies in its abandonment.

As at all important centers in the park, you will find a naturalist program at Glacier Point, including campfire talks several nights a week and short guided trips in the daytime. Also, if you want to hike, you have ample opportunity from here.

HIKES JOHN MUIR LIKED. The year before automobiles were allowed in Yosemite National Park (1912), John Muir commended, in a chapter of a book,* several excursion routes to visitors who wanted to sample the scenic grandeur of Yosemite. Today most visitors ride an automobile into Yosemite Valley, yet the trails remain the finest avenues to travel if you wish to see Yosemite to best advantage. With Glacier Point as your base, you can turn several of the strenuous climbs into downhill hikes to the valley floor. Each of the three hikes described here could take most of the day. Be sure you've acclimated to the high altitude (at least half a day) before starting out.

Four-Mile Trail. From Glacier Point this trail zigzags down the canyon wall to the valley floor about 3½ miles west of Camp Curry. This is the shortest and steepest of the walks, and the distance is really about 4.9 miles.

You could hike this route in 2 hours, but you'll probably want to take longer. The view is an everchanging one, and there are some wonderfully sweeping panoramas of Yosemite Valley. Sentinel Rock looms bold and very black in the afternoon shade; and almost all the

*"How Best to Spend One's Yosemite Time," *The Yosemite* (The Century Company, 1912) continues to be an excellent trail guide. Footnotes in the paperbound reprint (Doubleday & Company, Inc., Garden City, N.Y., 1962; 95 cents) clarify or correct the details in the original publication that had become obsolete or inaccurate in the intervening years.

way down, the trail dips in and out of the sunlight every few hundred feet.

Panorama Trail. This is the old Glacier Point Trail, which leaves Glacier Point and drops down into Illilouette Canyon and on, ending eventually at Happy Isles. It covers the most varied terrain of the walks; every mile of the 8.3-mile route seems more interesting than the one before it. Sometimes you walk through the woods, amid greenness and shade, and sometimes you cross broad open spaces, with views that go back to dark canyons and out to shining peaks and burnished domes.

Half Dome comes into view again and again, changing in outline as you hike toward it. From Glacier Point, its sheer side stands out. Farther along the trail, you approach the rounded and deeply furrowed back of the dome.

The special surprise on this trail is the infrequently-seen waterfall, the Illilouette, in the canyon of the same name. There are fine views of Yosemite Falls in the distance, and then you hear—and later see—Nevada Fall. Viewed close up Nevada Fall has a hypnotic effect. Here the river flows out from a dark pool to plunge over the ledge in a white fury of spray for 594 feet, and then cascades into Emerald Pool. At the top of Nevada Fall there are flat, sun-warmed rocks with plenty of space for picnicking at a safe distance from the precipice.

At trail junctions from Nevada Fall, take the trail to the right each time. The distance is slightly shorter, and it's a prettier route. Part of it goes down the stone steps of the Mist Trail, wet from Vernal Fall and very welcome on a warm day, as you head toward the end of the trail at Happy Isles, not far away.

Pohono Trail. This beautiful trail follows along the rim, more or less paralleling it for almost the full length of the valley, descending at about the Wawona Tunnel, and coming onto the valley floor in the vicinity of Bridalveil Fall. The entire length of the trail is about 12 miles, but you can take as much of it as you choose. In June and early July, it is one of the loveliest wildflower walks in Yosemite. However, there's much to recommend it any time from spring through fall. From Sentinel Dome on your way, you get one of the best wide angle views of Yosemite. Farther along are the geological features known as the Fissures. These giant clefts give an effect of wedges cut into the Yosemite wall to reveal a cross section of its structure. Listen to hear how many times your echo will bounce back to you. One of the Pohono Trail's finest aspects is the view of El Capitan. From Taft Point, and farther on at Dewey Point, this great landmark looms up right across from you along the rim of the narrow portion of the valley.

To shorten this hike: Start from the parking loop at the base of Sentinel Dome, eliminating the steep climb on the first mile of the trail. Or you might cut 3½ miles by starting from the lateral that leaves Glacier Point Road about 2½ miles from the hotel and goes out to Taft Point.

Near the end of this trail, there is a short, steep alternate which brings you to the road at the east end of Wawona Tunnel. The longer, more gradual descent follows the old Inspiration Point Road for 1½ miles and joins the main road 1.2 miles east of the tunnel entrance.

For trail guides and for identification purposes, take the U.S.G.S. maps, *Yosemite Valley* and *Yosemite National Park*. Each costs 50 cents at the visitor center and other map sources.

If you need a ride back to Glacier Point, it is often possible to find a volunteer at the hotel desk to drive your car to the trail end. Another way is to drive your car there the day before you take a hike, then take the bus back to Glacier Point. It leaves Camp Curry daily at 1:45 P.M.

Tuolumne Meadows

To many people the choicest section of Yosemite is Tuolumne Meadows. Here you are at the gateway to the High Country—this largest and one of the most beautiful of the sub-Alpine meadows in the entire Sierra lies at an elevation of 8,600 feet.

This is a much different place from the valley; there are no dances, no golf, no tennis; it is appreciated in a

FOUR-MILE TRAIL is short, steep, spectacular. Switchbacks afford sweeping views of Yosemite Valley.

RIDERS AND PACK TRAINS in the High Country meander through wide meadows and granite outcrops from Tuolumne Meadows down to Glen Aulin. Here the going is easy along the upper Tuolumne River.

much different way. Those who know the area return again and again, arriving with a sense of relief at leaving the crowds behind. Newcomers soon learn to appreciate the clear sparkling air, the freedom from noise, the feeling of spaciousness, and the atmosphere of informality.

Tuolumne Meadows is about 55 miles from Yosemite Valley, about a 1½-hour trip. It is 40 miles from Big Oak Flat Entrance Station or, if you enter from the east by Tioga Pass, it is 21 miles from Lee Vining.

The 40-odd miles from Big Oak Flat to Tioga Pass (9,941 feet) is a fine road with wide sweeping curves and scenic vistas. Part of this road is new, replacing an early-day mining road which was narrow and winding and meandered around obstacles instead of going over or through them. The National Park Service has retained two short sections of the old road for historical reasons. It should be understood that these are side roads and not thoroughfares. They are described in the handy booklet *Self-guiding Auto Tour of Yosemite National Park*, which may be purchased in the Village. Here from Tuolumne Meadows and Tioga Road is probably the best accessible lake and stream fishing in the park. If you are lucky enough to get a campsite on the river, you can catch fish right in front of your tent.

The ranger naturalists hold campfire programs several nights each week at the campground and conduct daily nature walks and hikes afield. Visitors are always welcome at the small museum and information office at the edge of the campground near the store.

All in all, Tuolumne Meadows is a delightful spot to spend a few days, a week, a month. If you are looking for convenience but no luxuries, people but no crowds, and plenty to do that makes a national park vacation worthwhile, then you need look no further.

THE HIGH SIERRA LOOP. Tuolumne Meadows is the main stop on the trail of 50 miles that is commonly referred to as the High Sierra Loop. There are six camps on the loop. From Tuolumne, they are Tuolumne Meadows Camp (8,600 feet), Glen Aulin Camp (7,800 feet), May Lake Camp (9,270 feet), Sunrise Camp (9,400 feet), Merced Lake Camp (7,100 feet), Vogelsang Camp (10,000 feet), and then back to the Tuolumne Meadows Camp. The camps are spaced about a day's hike apart (about 10 miles), and provide good food, lodging in tents, showers, and close proximity to good fishing spots. They are a boon for the hiker who doesn't want to carry a 40-pound pack of food and equipment. The camps are open only in the summer, and rates (about $10.00 per person) include meals.

Each Monday morning from about July 1 to August 28, a ranger naturalist guide starts out with a group on the Seven-Day High Sierra Trip, stopping at the High Sierra Camps. The rate of about $67.00 includes the guide service, lodgings in dormitory-type tents, and breakfast and dinner. Groups are limited to 15 persons. Children from 12 to 18 may go when accompanied by an adult, but do not go on reduced fare. A deposit is required; make reservations early.

Twice a week during the same season, the company offers six-day guided saddle trips from the valley to the High Sierra Camps. Groups are limited to 10 persons with a 10-pound baggage limit each; and the total cost, including lodging and meals, is about $119. Four-day saddle trips departing each Wednesday from Tuolumne Meadows cost about $76.00.

It is not necessary to go with a party, although they offer fun and good fellowship. You can go by yourself, stopping over as long as you wish at each camp to rest, fish, or explore the country. Either way, you should make advance reservations with the Yosemite Park and Curry Co., Yosemite National Park, California 95389.

There are many interesting spots, reached by short or long hikes, out of Tuolumne Meadows. The naturalist or one of the rangers will be glad to discuss the possibilities with you.

YOSEMITE IN WINTER

When the winter storms leave a deep cover of snow in the High Sierra, a visit to Yosemite Valley is especially rewarding. Drifts limn the ledges and creases of the valley walls, bringing into relief Yosemite's grand design. A mantle of white lies over roads, walks, and meadows; the snow caps fence posts and road signs, door lintels, window sills, rooftops, and chimneys.

VIEWS OF THE VALLEY

A view of the entire Yosemite Valley is magnificent, and it also helps familiarize you with the park's landmarks. In addition to Glacier Point itself, there are other awesome and easily reached vantage points from the Glacier Point area.

Sentinel Dome. For one of the finest views of Yosemite Valley, take the road to Sentinel Dome and walk up to its 8,122-foot summit. You are nearly 1,000 feet higher than the Glacier Point Lookout and almost directly across from Yosemite Falls. Half Dome seems little more than arm's length away. No other vantage point with a far-reaching view of the valley is within such a short and not-too-steep hiking distance of a roadside parking area.

Spring is a spectacular time for this view. Waterfalls are in full volume; streams are flowing full, fast, and noisily; and the lingering snows have limned the valley landmarks—El Capitan, Half Dome, Royal Arches—with ridges of white emphasizing their grandeur.

Sentinel Dome is reached by a spur that leaves the main road less than 2 miles from the Glacier Point Hotel. You can drive within 300 yards of the top, or you can walk the whole distance from the hotel in less than an hour. There is no precise trail—you just scramble up the gray granite dome.

Be sure you take a map of Yosemite when you climb Sentinel Dome; it will help you identify the peaks, spires, rivers, and waterfalls in your view. And notice the often-photographed Jeffrey pine growing right out of the granite on top.

Point Overlook. Few views of Yosemite Valley are more dramatic than that from Taft Point. It is on the south rim of the valley, only about 2 miles west of Glacier Point, and close to the interesting geological formations known as The Fissures, a series of deep, narrow clefts in Profile Cliff to the east.

The outlook is a favorite stopping-off place along the Pohono Trail between Glacier Point and Wawona Tunnel. For an easy look, drive the Glacier Point Road to its intersection with the Pohono Trail, and walk the trail a mile or so north to Taft Point.

TAFT POINT gives thrilling view of valley, high country, and El Capitan directly opposite.

mercury will stand around 45 degrees or higher, while at night it will drop to 25 degrees or lower. The valley usually gets about 90 inches of snowfall throughout the winter months, with long periods of clear, bright weather between storms. Here there are two extremes of winter climate. The north side of the valley receives full benefit of the sun, and the cliffs reflect and radiate this warmth so that the snow melts quickly and the weather is relatively balmy. The shady south side, however, is usually covered with snow from December to March. At a higher elevation, the ski area at Badger Pass enjoys ideal conditions for winter sports.

Special winter tours operate to take you sightseeing in Yosemite Valley, the ski area, and Mariposa Grove.

The Arch Rock Entrance, on the all-year highway (State 140), the South Entrance (State 41), and the Big Oak Flat Entrance (State 120) remain open in the winter. The Park Service keeps the roads free from snow in the valley as well as to the South Entrance and Badger Pass. Although they may not be needed on your winter visit, bring tire chains, for you may awake some morning to a fall of fresh snow 6 to 8 inches deep.

TWO WALKS IN THE SNOW. To be a part of winter Yosemite, get out on your own where it is all around you. These two short walks can be negotiated easily during winter months.

Mirror Lake to Snow Creek Bridge. This is a comparatively easy 3-mile hike with a gradual climb, starting at the Mirror Lake parking lot. Take the trail up the north side of Tenaya Canyon until you come to the bridge just below Snow Creek Falls. Cross the creek here, and walk back down the sunny south side of the canyon. Another bridge crosses Tenaya Creek. Double back about 1/5 mile to Mirror Lake.

Camp 4 to Columbia Point. This one is shorter but steeper, a mile altogether up and back. Walk from Camp 4 to the base of the valley wall and pick up Yosemite Falls Trail. (Trail signs are sometimes removed by December; ask for directions if you are not familiar with this trail.) The ascent to Columbia Point is by a south-facing, sunny trail; return the same way.

Winter Activities

Badger Pass is the oldest organized ski area in the Sierra. It is 20 miles from the valley on Glacier Point Road and is usually open mid-December to early April. Since there are no overnight facilities, you may "commute" from the valley by car or bus. The Ski House at the Pass offers quick meals with indoor or outdoor dining.

Badger Pass accommodates varied abilities. There is a gentle slope with a T-bar lift for beginners; and T-bars and a double chair lift are located on other slopes of varying steepness. Cross-country trails, marked and maintained by the Park Service, take you away from the more populated slopes.

FOR SKATERS, the outdoor rink at Curry Village is open afternoons and evenings all through the winter.

It is very quiet. Everyday noises are muffled, and as you walk, you become aware of other sounds—the distant boom and thunder of waterfalls from rivers running high, the whisper of snow falling from laden branches, the drip-drip-drip of water from icicles melting in the afternoon sun.

The valley's popularity as a winter resort is growing each year. It offers good skiing, snowshoeing, and skating; most of its facilities are operating; it is easily accessible; and the climate is ideal.

Snowfall is greatest during January, February, and March; and while January is the coldest month, temperatures are not extreme. In the valley at midday, the

Ski classes and special classes for children are held each day at Badger Pass, and there is even a babysitting service while parents are away on the slopes. A snowmobile will take you sightseeing around the high country. It leaves hourly from the Ski House. Cost is $2.00 per person.

For those who enjoy ice skating, there is a large outdoor rink at Curry Village, open weekdays from 2 until 10 P.M., and on weekends and holidays from 8 A.M. until 10 P.M. Rental skates are available at the rink. Snowshoeing is popular with some. You may bring your own or rent them at Badger Pass. You can also rent sleds and snow saucers at Curry Village.

Many people who are not interested in any winter sport go to Yosemite during the snow season. They go because they enjoy snow (many California children come here who have never seen snow). And they go because the air is crisp and the valley is beautiful, and because the smell of wood smoke on a winter evening brings back memories.

No one will criticize your snowtime lethargy. It is pleasant to relax in front of a big fireplace at The Ahwahnee or the Lodge and watch a storm through huge wide windows. And it is a thrill to awake some morning to a new world—made fresh and clean by a white blanket which fell while you slept.

Where to Stay in the Winter

In the valley, Yosemite Lodge remains open during the winter months, as do many housekeeping cabins. The Ahwahnee Hotel is also open, except for a short period in December when it is closed for renovations. The highlight of Christmas Day and the season at The Ahwahnee is the annual Bracebridge Dinner, a pageant based on Washington Irving's account in his *Sketch Book* of a typical Yorkshire Christmas dinner during the reign of George III. All the characters of the book are present in costume and all the wondrous dishes described by Irving—the baron of beef, the peacock pie, the boar's head, the wassail, and the pudding—are presented formally to the Squire of Bracebridge Manor. This ceremonious dinner has become extremely popular, and if you ever hope to attend, make reservations at least 12 months in advance. Make reservations early, too, for a place to stay in Yosemite during Christmas holidays.

WHITE MAGIC OF SNOW in Yosemite emphasizes grandeur of park features from huge Half Dome to individual trees. For a few days after winter storm, snow conceals marks left by warm-weather crowds.

SEQUOIA & KINGS CANYON NATIONAL PARKS

Groves of Big Trees and never-ending High Country wilderness

FROM TOP OF MOUNT WHITNEY, *highest point in United States outside Alaska, view to northwest of vast Kern River Basin, where peaks jut in all directions, is characteristic of these two mountain parks.*

SEQUOIA AND KINGS CANYON National Parks, located next to each other along the ridge of the Sierra Nevada, share many natural features, and are administered as one park. Each contains several thousand acres of the largest trees on earth, the giant sequoias, and encompasses a hiker's domain of spectacular peaks and canyons threaded with an intricate trail system.

Sequoia, the first national park in California and the second one in the entire system, was established to protect its groves of giant sequoias, found here in greater abundance than anywhere else on earth. Sequoia contains the highest mountain in the United States, outside of Alaska, and is a year-around park.

In Kings Canyon National Park, it seems that nature has purposely arranged the topography to guard the rugged beauty for only those willing to exert themselves. This is a trail park, and unless you take some of the 388 miles of trail on foot or horseback, you will miss the most spectacular sections.

How to Get There

Sequoia and Kings Canyon are adjoining parks in the Sierra Nevada.

BY CAR: The shortest route to the parks from the north is through Fresno over State Highway 180. From Fresno to the Big Stump Entrance of Kings Canyon Park is 52 miles. From the south, enter through Visalia either over State 69 to Big Stump Entrance or State 198 to Ash Mountain Entrance of Sequoia National Park.

The scenic, all-year Generals Highway connects the two parks and the two largest trees, General Grant in Grant Grove and General Sherman in Giant Forest.

BY BUS, RAIL, AND AIR: In the summer the park's concessioner buses meet Continental and Greyhound buses and Southern Pacific trains at Tulare, and Greyhound buses also at Visalia. Concessioner buses transport passengers to Giant Forest in Sequoia; holders of reservations at Grant Grove Lodge can obtain transportation there on the regular sightseeing tour. If you make your trip off-season, usually between mid-September and late May, make reservations and have them confirmed in advance for transportation to the parks.

United Airlines serves Visalia, and United, Pacific, and Trans World Airlines serve Fresno. There are no connections from Fresno to the parks.

Where to Stay

Accommodations at Sequoia and Kings Canyon are not as pretentious as in some parks. Rustic cabins in perfect keeping with the sequoias that tower above them coexist with new modern accommodations. Campgrounds are numerous, well equipped, and located in strategic and beautiful spots throughout both parks.

GIANT FOREST LODGE in Sequoia's Giant Forest Village is a fitting and unflamboyant showpiece. One-room cottages scattered among Big Trees have a rustic motif, yet the window-walled dining room borders on sumptuousness. You can stay at the Lodge for about $15.00 for two persons. Canvas-top cabins are lower in price. The Lodge is open from late May to mid-October; cottages remain open until late October.

CAMP KAWEAH at Giant Forest also has motel-type units and a coffee shop nearby. The camp is open all year, and prices compare with those at the Lodge.

Housekeeping accommodations are available at Camp Kaweah and the Lodge in clean and comfortable cabins complete with firewood. Rates are reasonable at around $10.50 for two persons.

GRANT GROVE LODGE in Kings Canyon, at an elevation of 6,600 feet, operates on the European plan; meals are served at the nearby coffee shop. Cottage with bath is $15.00 for two persons.

MEADOW CAMP in Grant Grove offers housekeeping accommodations including linens in cabins without baths. Rates compare with Camp Kaweah.

CEDAR GROVE CAMP, farther north in Kings Canyon National Park, contains a limited number of canvas-top cabins available on a first-come first-served basis.

You should make advance reservations for lodges and cabins and send a deposit. Write to Sequoia and Kings Canyon National Parks Co., Sequoia National Park, California 93262.

CAMPGROUNDS are strategically placed throughout Sequoia National Park, six in the vicinity of Giant Forest, and four at lower elevations. The largest is Lodgepole, 4 miles north of Giant Forest, with 317 campsites. Dorst Creek, 8 miles beyond, is next in size. These camps will accommodate house trailers. The campgrounds at higher elevations (about 6,400 feet) are open from mid-May until early September, depending on snow conditions. Lodgepole generally remains open the longest.

At the lower elevations, Potwisha Trailer Camp, just inside the Ash Mountain Entrance, and Buckeye Flat, 3 miles beyond, are open the year around and are well equipped. You can leave your trailer at either of these for an easier drive on the hills ahead and a relatively warm place to return for the night. Two other low elevation campgrounds, South Fork and Atwell Mill, are small and close by November 1.

In Kings Canyon National Park there are eight well-equipped campgrounds, four at Cedar Grove and four at Grant Grove. Azalea campground at Grant Grove and Camps 3 and 4 at Cedar Grove have designated areas for house trailers.

HISTORY

The Indians of the Kaweah River drainage knew the Big Trees long before settlers moved into the San Joaquin Valley during the middle of the last century.

Hale Tharp, a settler who went beyond Visalia to run cattle near Three Rivers, was apparently a friendly sort,

MAGNIFICENT SEQUOIAS *overwhelm the small boy looking at them close up. This group of mature sequoias in Giant Forest, The Cloister, forms natural enclosure that is gradually filling with young firs.*

for he was soon on good terms with the Indians, especially their chief, Chappo. One day in 1858, they took him beyond Moro Rock where he saw the sequoia groves of Giant Forest. He was the first white man to see the Big Trees.

Later Tharp spent his summers there in a huge hollow log near Crescent Meadow. John Muir, one of the strongest advocates of preserving the trees, stayed several days as Tharp's guest in what he called the "noble den." The log remains today as a small exhibit and is much as it was when Tharp occupied it.

Muir named Giant Forest, but James Wolverton, a trapper, discovered its largest tree and named it for his Civil War commander, William T. Sherman.

At an early date, public spirited citizens and conservationists became alarmed at the rapidly expanding lumber activities moving nearer and nearer the Big Trees. One of the last straws was the establishment of a sawmill about 9 miles from Giant Forest.

The result of their efforts was in favor of the aesthetic, and on September 25, 1890, President Harrison signed the bill that created Sequoia as the country's second national park and removed the last threat to the finest grove of trees in the world. In 1926 Sequoia National Park was enlarged from its original 252 square miles to its present 604 square miles.

Kings Canyon has the distinction of being one of the oldest yet one of the youngest national parks. A part of the present Kings Canyon National Park came under government protection as early as 1890, three weeks after Sequoia was established, but the rest was not included until 50 years later. The original section, known as General Grant National Park, is now the General Grant Grove.

The Kings Canyon area had been proposed for park status long before the idea was realized. John Muir campaigned for it in 1891, and the issue was reopened in 1926 at the time Sequoia's size was more than doubled. Kings Canyon National Park was finally established March 4, 1940.

The park takes its name from the river, named by a Spanish explorer in 1805 for the Three Wise Men—*El Rio de los Santos Reyes*, the River of the Holy Kings.

NATURAL FEATURES

In general, the geology of Sequoia and Kings Canyon is the same as that of Yosemite, for all are part of the Sierra Nevada.

The Sierra Nevada itself is a great block of the earth's crust which, over millions of years, was tilted—sharply

THE BIG TREES

Within the groves of Sequoia and Kings Canyon national parks stand several thousand giant sequoias (*Sequoiadendron giganteum*), largest of all living things and among the oldest.

The General Sherman is the largest tree in the world. It is 102 feet in base circumference, and 120 feet above the ground the trunk is still 17 feet through. There is a limb 140 feet up on the Sherman that is 6.8 feet in diameter, thicker than most forest trees. Yet, even at a towering 272 feet, the Sherman's height does not top others in the sequoia genus (among the coast redwoods, some trees have been known to grow over 400 feet high).

Second place in size is given to Kings Canyon's General Grant Tree, with a base circumference actually 6 feet larger than the Sherman's but with a smaller total volume. Next are the Boole and Hart trees. If there are any larger than these measured trees, they would have to be in southern Sequoia National Park or to the south in Sequoia National Forest, where there are groves big enough and remote enough to conceal a possible challenger.

The huge General Sherman Tree in Giant Forest and General Grant Tree in Kings Canyon were standing in the Bronze Age, more than 3,000 years ago. The Sherman was probably a healthy seedling when Egypt's Old Kingdom was at its height; it was pretty well along in its youth when Rome was founded; and it was much as you see it today when Columbus discovered the New World.

The sequoias are old geologically, too. Fossil remains tell us they were well distributed over the earth during the Age of Reptiles. Of the many related species, it is believed that all are extinct except the giant sequoia and the coast redwood (*Sequoia sempervirens*) in this hemisphere, and the so-called dawn redwood (*Metasequoia glyptostroboides*) located in China. The genus was named by an Austrian botanist for Sequoyah, inventor of the Cherokee alphabet.

It is thought that almost all the sequoias were destroyed during the Ice Age and that the remaining ones exist today only because they were lucky enough to have ancestors that grew in spots where the glaciers did not reach. Most of those remaining are within these two national parks and adjoining forests.

There are several reasons for the long life of a sequoia. The bark is extremely thick and almost impervious to fire. In addition, the bark contains much tannin which discourages insects. With the threat of these two enemies lessened, the sequoias are well ahead of other trees in natural protection. They also seem to have remarkable vitality and recuperative powers, so that when a tree is occasionally scorched or even badly burned by a forest fire, the wound heals relatively quickly.

Man, therefore, has been the greatest enemy of these giants. The extensive groves today don't begin to match the vast sequoia forest that was still intact just a century ago. Between 1862 and 1900, logging operations wiped out the finest forest in the world, containing at least two trees—and possible four or more—that may have been even bigger than the General Sherman. Ironically, two of these giants were not cut for their

MASSIVE SHELL of a burned-out Big Tree dwarfs the two small boys peering out of it.

wood, but simply so that sections of their trunks could be exhibited at two world's fairs. Today the threat of man is reduced as more and more of the great trees come under federal and state protection.

The enormous size of the sequoias is captured by the picture above. Massed together, the Big Trees seem in scale; but if you walk down the length of a fallen trunk, clamber through a tangle of upturned roots, or saunter through a hollow trunk, you will grasp the great proportions of these trees.

Wander then along some of the less frequented trails under the Big Trees and you will become a philosopher. New thoughts will come to you—new concepts of space and time, for one *feels* the age of these trees. Their size and age will humble you, yet the experience will give you hope in the realization that these trees have survived over three thousand years of war and famine, success and failure, and they continue to thrive and grow and propagate. Walk under the sequoias and your own cares and the cares of the modern world will seem but of the moment.

on the east and more gently on the west—and then sculptured by rains, winds, deep-cutting streams, and finally by great glaciers.

The mountain peaks of Sequoia and Kings Canyon seem endless. And they are high—many in Sequoia exceed 11,000 feet, and Mount Whitney reaches an elevation of 14,495 feet.

Plants and Animals

As would be expected in two adjoining areas, the plants and animals in Sequoia and Kings Canyon national parks are almost identical.

No matter which way you enter the two parks, you will be impressed by the changing vegetation as you gain elevation. When it is summer at the lower elevations, it is spring at Giant Forest and often winter in certain parts of the High Country. Spring is the flower time, but you will always find something in bloom. There are about 1,200 kinds of plants here.

In spring at the lower elevations, where the heat of summer comes early, you will find the California buckeye, the fremontia, the redbud (glorious color), and the chamise—flowers that must bloom and seed before the high temperatures affect them. Bush lupine will paint the roadsides with clumps of bright blue as will the great masses of ceanothus, whose fragrance you can breathe even from your car. Higher up, especially along streams, is the Pacific dogwood with its perfect, large, white blooms.

In meadows and other damp spots, you will find great beds of shooting stars nodding on their delicate stems, and you will see the bright yellow monkey flower. Harebells, bluebells, and Indian paint brush are all conspicuous as are corn lilies and cow parsnips.

An entire book could be written on the animals of these two parks, for there are many species to be found from the low elevation around Ash Mountain to the bare peaks of the High Country. The two largest animals that you may encounter are the American black bear and the California mule deer. Deer are frequently seen along the Generals Highway and often in the meadows at sunset. Infrequently seen, all bears in the park are black bears; the one of a lighter shade is the blond of the species. The danger of feeding or even getting near the animals is stressed often.

At the lower elevations, especially at night, you may see raccoon and the beautiful small gray fox. Most animals are shy, and you will probably see more of them at night by the lights of your car than you will in the daytime.

Throughout the forested area are weasels, marten, an occasional fisher, a rare wolverine. Coyotes are sometimes encountered in meadows where they hunt mice.

Bobcats and mountain lions are among the most human-shy of all the animals, and you can count yourself fortunate if you catch a glimpse of one.

In the High Country, mountain sheep are present, but seldom seen. The yellow-bellied marmot is fairly common; and more often heard than seen is the interesting little pika, a gray animal resembling a baby rabbit, that lives and whistles to you from the rough talus slopes. You may find his hayfield where he has cut grass and spread it out to dry on a flat rock for winter food.

There are about 194 different species of birds reported in the parks. Bluebirds are common. The gray dipper or water ouzel sings and bobs on the spray-drenched rocks of fast-flowing streams, and big golden eagles are frequently seen in the High Country.

If birds are of particular interest to you, be sure to take some of the nature walks with the ranger naturalists and attend the evening programs that frequently have discussions of them.

THE HIGH COUNTRY

For the three summer months of the year, the High Country of Sequoia and Kings Canyon, with its abundance of native wildlife, opens its 1,000 miles of trails to humans, who enter the wilderness their own way, for their own reasons—alone or with groups; for short hikes or packing in; to fish, to climb, or just to look and feel.

The John Muir Trail is the main artery through this country. Beginning in Yosemite, it runs south for 225 miles at high elevation to Whitney Portal, half of its route lying within Kings Canyon and Sequoia parks, where you find most of the true High Sierra. Named for the great conservationist who died just before construction started, the trail took 40 years to its completion in 1938. The superbly engineered High Sierra Trail, beginning at Crescent Meadow, will take you all the way to Mount Whitney (70 miles). A full network of supplementary trails within the two parks gives access to the full variety of High Sierra terrain: tall silent forests of fir and pine, knife-edged passes, glacier remnants, countless sparkling lakes, marshy alpine meadows splashed with wildflowers, and talus slopes where marmots sun themselves.

If you are planning a back country excursion, it is important to be familiar with the section on how to prepare for and enjoy a High Country adventure found in the introduction to this book. Many trips can be taken, some longer and more strenuous than others; a ranger station has full information. Here we describe some of the more popular hikes and trail entrances to this mountain wilderness—a new world.

Sequoia

Sequoia's High Country is impressive with its towering peaks, glacial lakes and streams, and the 2,000-foot-deep Kern Canyon, from which one wall rises 5,000 feet. The total picture is unequalled in grandeur.

ON BIGHORN PLATEAU back country travelers move along a tarn whose gravelly rim conceals the drop-off to Kern Canyon, but not the peaks of the Great Western Divide that rise beyond it.

This is trail country. Horses and pack stock are available near most of the entrances; trails are well marked, and there is plenty of fishing.

FROM THE WEST. A backpacking trip that is not too strenuous and takes you to fine groves of sequoias is from Crescent Meadow to Bearpaw Meadow and on 13 miles to Atwell Ranger Station. The most difficult climb on the trip is out of Redwood Meadow, but this is less than 2,000 feet and the balance is downhill. A few miles before the ranger station, the trail forks. If you prefer, the left fork goes to Silver City, an old mining town a mile up the road from your destination, and avoids the steep switchbacks that lead to Atwell. If you don't wish to hike back to Crescent Meadow, someone can bring your car to Atwell or Silver City.

Another beautiful trip in this locality continues beyond Bearpaw to scenic Hamilton Lake, up over Kaweah Gap with spectacular views, and down into Nine Lakes Basin (a total distance of about 10 miles). You can spend a day or two or even a week exploring the lakes in the basin area; there are plenty of camping sites and not too many people.

Also from Crescent Meadow, the High Sierra Trail will take you the full 70 miles to Mount Whitney. In and out of tall fir and pine forest and through hanging gardens of wildflowers, it contours along the south-facing side of the Middle Fork canyon and therefore opens early. The trail can also be a fine non-destination hike of any length you want.

Especially if you're staying at Giant Forest, you may be interested in two good hikes that leave from nearby Wolverton Meadow. One hike takes you to beautiful Pear Lake past three other small lakes; the longer, steeper hike culminating at Alta Peak provides you with some of the Sierra's grandest scenery.

The 7-mile hike to Pear Lake taps some choice scenery from 7,250 to 9,600 feet elevation, yet it is not considered a difficult trip.

At the fork in the trail, a mile and a half along the way, take the left fork to the north (the south one goes to Panther Gap and joins the trail to Alta Peak). In another mile and a half, you're near the Watchtower, a high, sheer, granite pinnacle. Here the scene suddenly snaps wide open. The exfoliated granite tableland at the head of Tokopah Valley spreads to the east; Mount Silliman is across the valley to the north; and just below you the sheer granite face of the Watchtower drops some 2,000 feet down to the valley floor.

Beyond the Watchtower, the trail hugs the face of the cliffs. At Heather Lake (9,300 feet) the steepest part is behind you. Over an easy ridge and down into a basin, the trail passes Aster and Emerald lakes set in granite pockets. The next mile, the last one and an easy climb, goes up to the northern end of Pear Lake, largest of the four small tarns. Like the others it is stocked with rainbow trout. Several small and pleasant camping spots are scattered along the shores of the lake.

The Alta Peak trip is a good choice for a long weekend when you haven't time to do a lot of exploring. It affords a sample of high country grandeur, with views to distant peaks and deep glacial-carved canyons. From the top to the east stand the giants of the Great Western Divide: Eagle Scout and Triple Divide peaks, Mount Stewart, and far off in the distance, Mount Whitney. To the south, the outlines of Sawtooth Peak and Farewell Gap dominate the view; and to the north, you look out to the drainage of the South Fork of the Kings River and Mount Silliman. Two U.S.G.S. topographic maps, *Triple Divide Peak, California* (a useful trail guide) and *Sequoia and Kings Canyon National Parks*, identify features more distant.

The trail to Alta Peak is steep and short, from 7,200 feet to 11,204 feet in the 8½ miles from Wolverton Meadow, and you will probably not meet many other hikers along the way. Though hardy hikers can make the trip in one long day, it is more pleasant in two days. Camping overnight on upper Mehrten Creek or Alta Meadow, you'll see flickering fires of campers far down the canyon at Hospital Rock and probably some deer nearby.

FROM THE SOUTH. For the backpacker there are many hiking possibilities from the Mineral King area. These are good trips for the fisherman. Like all trails out of Mineral King, the one over Franklin Pass is steep and made of granite sand. An overnight camp on one of the Franklin Lakes will break the climb. If you want, a packer at Mineral King will take you to the top. The grand view from this 11,400-foot pass on the Great Western Divide is reward for the climb.

For the lake fisherman, the trail that goes to the left a couple of miles below the pass leads a mile to the north to Little Forester Lake, where there are plenty of 8 and 9-inch brook trout. For the stream fisherman, Rattlesnake Creek, which the trail follows, is one of the best trout streams in the Sierra, with rainbows and rainbow-golden crosses up to 10 and 12 inches. Camping spots abound in this warm and sunny valley.

THE MOUNT WHITNEY CLIMB is not as strenuous as one would suppose, and hundreds of people of all ages reach the summit each year. Whitney can be approached from either the east or the west, and your choice may depend on how much time you have. Though it is more varied and scenic, the route from the west will take a minimum of 9 or 10 days; the one from the east 2 or 3 days.

From the west take the trail from Crescent Meadow to Kaweah Gap, down into Big Arroyo, and up on Chagoopa Plateau. After crossing the plateau, the trail descends into Upper Funston Meadow on the Kern River and follows on an easy grade to Wallace Creek. About 3 miles up Wallace Creek, it turns south to Crabtree

Meadow then goes up Whitney Creek to Trail Crest and on to the summit.

If you have the time, the western approaches are to be desired because they take you through a great variety of beautiful and spectacular country. By going this way, you can see the High Country of Sequoia and climb Mount Whitney on the same trip. You can make a circle trip, returning by one of several routes; or you can go back on the east side, having made arrangements to be picked up at Whitney Portal.

From the east you can drive to the beginning of the Mount Whitney trail by turning off U.S. Highway 395 at Lone Pine and driving 12 miles to the trail head at Whitney Portal (8,300 feet). Ahead is a hike of 13 miles and a climb of 6,000 feet. The trail is new and well kept. Many other hikers use the same pass (Trail Crest, 13,400 feet) to get into the back country.

Horses are available at Whitney Portal, and the round trip to the summit can be made in a day on horseback. The round trip can be made in one day on foot if you are an able mountain traveler, but it is much wiser to

HIGH COUNTRY HIKING along the Alta Peak Trail takes you to some of the Sierra's grandest scenery.

take two days. There are two or three lakes stretched out at convenient intervals above Whitney Portal. If you camp at one, you can make an early start the next morning and get back to camp at a reasonable hour that evening. Even this will give you a day's hike of 20 miles, but half of it will be downhill. There is water along most of the route except the last 4 or 5 miles where there is no water and little vegetation.

Climbing Mount Whitney is an adventure in itself, but don't discount the rewarding views that await you along the way and from the lofty summit. From nearly 15,000 feet, you can look along the crest of the Sierra, and even see the far-distant peaks of the Great Western Divide.

MANY HIGH SIERRA RIVERS like the Middle Fork of the Kings cascade down deep, V-shaped gorges.

Kings Canyon

Kings Canyon is the trail park. By studying your topographical map (a prerequisite for trail exploring), you will see 11 trail entrances to the park exclusive of the many trails that cross the common boundary between Kings Canyon and Sequoia. With such an elaborate trail system, it is possible to enter at any of the 11 points and eventually visit any spot you wish, but that is not the best way to explore the High Country. Note that trails from the east are short and steep. Trail mileages are greater from the west, but ascent is more gradual.

Four of the more popular trail entrances, approachable by car, are discussed here, along with a few trips and points of interest for each. Except for Cedar Grove all are on the eastern side of the park. Remember that Kings Canyon is a tremendous country; it would take many vacations to cover it with any degree of thoroughness.

KINGS CANYON. More people start into these mountains from Cedar Grove in the canyon of the Kings River than from any other point, probably because one of the park's two developed areas is near the beginning of the trail.

The Copper Creek Trail to Granite Pass and Simpson Meadow starts at the big parking area at Roads End and heads due north up Copper Creek. It is a steady climb to Granite Pass—from 5,000 to 10,000 feet in elevation—and the distance is 12 miles. Unless you are in good condition, this trip would be a tough one to start on walking; it would be better to let horses do the work. When you reach Granite Basin, roughly halfway to Simpson Meadow, you can see great expanses of bare granite and many little lakes. There is good fishing in most of the lakes from here on. Granite Pass, at the far end of the basin, is only 600 feet higher, and there the route is comparatively level or downhill through wooded country to Simpson Meadow. Almost every back country traveler in the park visits Simpson Meadow at one time or another. It is a lovely spot on the Middle Fork of the Kings River, a few miles above beautiful Blue Canyon and Tehipite Valley. A summer ranger station is located here. By planning a week by horse for this trip, you can spend two days on the trail each way and two or three days at the Meadow.

Another trail from Roads End is the Paradise Valley Trail which continues up the main river from the Copper Creek parking area. For a beautiful circle trip (four days by horse or a week backpacking) through the Sixty Lakes Basin, Rae Lakes, and Charlotte Lake Country, take this trail one way and the Bubbs Creek Trail from the east end of the Kings Canyon the other way. During this 43-mile round trip, there are dozens of spots where you can spend extra time. The Paradise Valley and Woods Creek portions of this loop trip are delightful—the trail is along the stream much of the way, and there is fairly good fishing in the deep pools. You will find ideal camping spots in tiny meadows and wooded sections.

The Bubbs Creek Trail, already mentioned as a good

THE JOHN MUIR TRAIL here is a deep groove worn by hikers and pack animals over the years as it swings across the High Country wilderness just below the 12,000-foot Pinchot Pass.

return from the Rae Lakes area, is also the most popular trail out of the Kings Canyon. This is a cool trail mostly through woods which follows the river from Roads End. It takes about three days round trip backpacking or a long two days by horse.

KEARSARGE PASS is classed as one of the better entrances to the High Country from the east side. By leaving U.S. 395 at Independence, you can reach the trail head at Onion Valley. From the pack base here, animals may be rented, and pack trains start into the High Country. The trail follows Pine Creek for part of the way and passes four small lakes, so there is plenty of water, but shade is scarce. It is a little over 4 miles to the top of Kearsarge, and you will probably meet other hikers as this is one of the most popular approaches.

The Kearsarge Lakes, Bullfrog Lake, and Charlotte Lake are 2 miles away in a basin that can be the starting point of many trips both long and short. A brisk climb of about 1,000 feet will take you to Glen Pass on the John Muir Trail 1½ miles to the north. The pass is the gateway to the famous Rae Lakes-Sixty Lakes Basin country which lies at its northern base. Rae Lakes stretch for over a mile in a long narrow valley in the middle of which rises the striking landmark Fin Dome. Beyond Rae Lakes is a series of smaller lakes, part of the headwaters of the South Fork of Woods Creek. The whole valley, with scattered clumps of trees and lots of water, is beautiful and has plenty of campsites. The

Sixty Lakes Basin lies directly west over the 500-foot ridge that forms the western wall of the valley. Since this region is off the main trail, it is not so heavily used as Rae Lakes Valley. The basin, dotted by sparkling lakes, offers good fishing and attractive spots to camp.

For another good trip from the Charlotte Lake area, follow the main trail south about 1½ miles to Vidette Meadows. Then leave the trail and follow up Vidette Creek to the beautiful lakes of the same name which lie in a granite basin between East and West Vidette peaks. You can make this round trip in one day. Another excellent trip which will take a day each way leads you into the Gardiner Lakes Basin at the foot of Mount Gardiner to the northwest. This area is well off the well-traveled routes and is attractive in the solitude it offers. The trail follows the outlet of Charlotte Lake for about a mile, then begins a long and scenic climb to a pass above the basin. There are golden trout in the lakes.

For a longer trip, you can use the Bullfrog Lake area as a starting point for the loop described with the Paradise Valley Trail out of Cedar Grove, going either down Bubbs Creek or over Glen Pass and down Woods Creek.

TABOOSE PASS. The road to the trail over Taboose Pass leaves U.S. Highway 395 about 14 miles north of Independence and ends on the north side of Taboose Creek. The Taboose Pass entrance is probably the least traveled of the four described in this book—probably because it leads to a rugged 7-mile climb to the Pass. In this distance you climb 6,200 feet, and it is not until the trail crosses Taboose Creek at the 8,500-foot level that water is available. Though pack stock can be taken over this trail, they will find it rough. After crossing Taboose Creek, the trail becomes more scenic; you will long remember the view from the Pass into the South Fork of the Kings River. After a 2-mile descent, you join the John Muir Trail, the main thoroughfare in the High Country. Nearby, intersecting the John Muir Trail from the west, is the trail that comes in from Cartridge Pass and the Simpson Meadow country beyond.

Fascinating country radiates out in all directions on practically level ground from the junction of these trails, and you can easily spend a week exploring and fishing the many lakes and the network of streams.

About a mile south on the John Muir Trail, the trail to Bench Lake cuts to the west. This scenic trip of 2½ miles runs along the valley rim of the South Fork of the Kings. Bench Lake is a beautiful body of water perched at the far end of a long level plateau. It is a popular spot with those who know this section and you may not be alone here, but the lake is large and there are plenty of scenic camping sites.

Another fine trip from the trail junction mentioned above also takes you south along the John Muir Trail, but continues on past the Bench Lake Trail to Lake Marjorie. This beautiful lake is situated in a long, comparatively level basin, with small lakes both above and below it. If you are feeling ambitious when you reach Lake Marjorie (a 2½-mile trip), continue on for another 2 miles to the top of Pinchot Pass, a climb of less than 1,000 feet with only the last part being very strenuous. The extra effort is rewarded by the spectacular view into the headwaters of Woods Creek.

Again from the trail junction, go north a mile on the John Muir Trail. You will find yourself at the lower end of a delightful glacial basin 2 or 3 miles long, dotted with small lakes connected by many small streams. Attractive campsites are plentiful, especially at the lower end where there is more timber. If you spend a couple of days exploring this area, you will probably want to see what is beyond Mather Pass at the basin's northern end. The zigzag trail leading to the top of the pass is long, but climbs less than 500 feet. From the top, you can look north into the headwaters of Palisade Creek and to the huge North and Middle Palisade peaks beyond. To the southeast, dominating the basin from which you have climbed, is Split Mountain (also known as the South Palisade). All three of these magnificent peaks rise to over 14,000 feet.

BISHOP PASS. Also from the east, the Bishop Pass entrance is one of the most beautiful approaches to the High Country of Kings Canyon National Park. The trail to the Pass is outstanding, and the country beyond, with the famous Evolution Valley in the northern section of the park, is a favorite area among those who know the Sierra best.

Inquire at Bishop on U.S. 6-395 for the road up Bishop Creek to South Lake. About 14 miles from Bishop, above the power plant, take the left fork of the road to its terminus at South Lake 7 miles beyond. Accommodations and supplies may be obtained at two points in this last 7 miles—at Andrews Camp Lodge and at Rainbow Lodge, at South Lake. Horses, pack animals, and guide service are also available.

The 7-mile trail over Bishop Pass starts at South Lake, elevation 9,750 feet, and ascends the 2,250 feet gradually except for a short, steep section at the end. The scenery is outstanding. Beginning with South Lake, a chain of sparkling lakes extends almost to the summit. These lie in a great glacial cirque hemmed in by towering cliffs and peaks.

From Bishop Pass a 2-mile trail drops to Dusy Lakes. This is the first good place to camp, and the several lakes in this basin are worth exploring and good for fishing. Less than a mile farther, the trail passes the lower end of another small basin also containing small lakes.

Three miles beyond Dusy Lakes, the trail intersects the John Muir Trail as it comes down from the Evolution Valley country. By turning right and going up the John Muir Trail for half a mile, you come to Little Pete Meadow, a favorite stopping point for trail parties. A half mile beyond is another small meadow south of the trail where you will find more wood and probably fewer people. Try fishing the stream here, which is the Middle Fork of the Kings.

What you do from this point depends upon your own inclinations. An easy trip of 7 miles down the John Muir Trail (south), past Grouse Meadow and up Palisade Creek brings you to beautiful Deer Meadow, where there is plenty of wood, water, fish, and refreshing scenery. You can spend a lot of time here, relaxing or getting a workout by following the trail farther toward Mather Pass.

Another choice is the 6-mile trip up the trail (north) to Muir Pass. You can camp at several small lakes, but the higher you go, the less wood you will find. It is not an easy 6 miles to the Pass (a 3,000-foot climb), but the top is the gateway to the famous Evolution Country and some of the most spectacular scenery in the Sierra. At the Pass a stone shelter built by the Sierra Club in memory of John Muir stands for the use of anyone caught there in a storm. You will probably find a supply of wood but don't use it unless you have to, and then replenish the supply for those who will follow you.

It would not be feasible here to map trails that should be taken beyond Muir Pass. This is a big country, and you could spend weeks exploring it. Parts of it are as rugged, barren, and harsh as the granite which composes it, yet there is beauty in this ruggedness. And parts of it are filled with another kind of beauty—the soft beauty of delightful meadows, singing streams, and sparkling lakes. This is the incomparable kind of country for which this great park was formed and is devotedly preserved and enjoyed today.

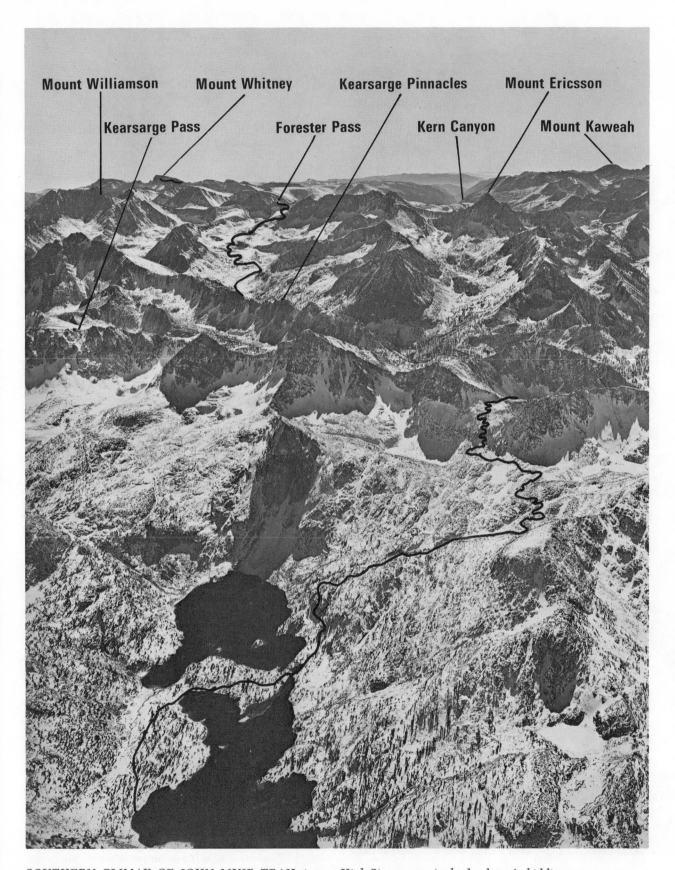

Mount Williamson   Mount Whitney   Kearsarge Pinnacles   Mount Ericsson

Kearsarge Pass   Forester Pass   Kern Canyon   Mount Kaweah

SOUTHERN CLIMAX OF JOHN MUIR TRAIL is true High Sierra, seemingly desolate, forbidding expanse of granite cliffs and basins. Trail skirts Rae Lakes, disappears over Glen Pass, climbs Mount Whitney.

ALREADY GIANTS, *young sequoias crowd into Causeway Meadow near Giant Forest in Sequoia National Park.*

SEQUOIA NATIONAL PARK

Of the national parks, Sequoia has remained little affected by human use. Unspoiled and natural, it offers a refreshing atmosphere for its visitors.

The southern entrance to the park through Ash Mountain is headquarters for both Sequoia and Kings Canyon national parks. However, the center of activity is the Giant Forest region, 16 miles north along the Generals Highway.

Schedules for free naturalist programs are posted in visitor centers and campgrounds throughout the park. During the summer months talks are given nightly around campfires in some of the major campgrounds as well as at the outdoor amphitheater across the road from Giant Forest Lodge, and daytime walks are conducted by naturalists. The visitor center at Lodgepole has exhibits and a slide program on the sequoias.

Ash Mountain

The southern entrance at Ash Mountain is the beginning of the beautiful Generals Highway into the park and the starting point for other interesting trips as well. The route of this nearly naturalized road winding up the hill toward Giant Forest was completed in 1926. A hint of the care taken of the natural scene is Tunnel Rock, a great boulder left in place to span the road.

At Hospital Rock 6 miles inside the present park boundary, Indians lived in the shelter of another huge boulder. Legend has it that this boulder was a spot to which the sick were brought for healing. Later, injured pioneers who took refuge under it called it Hospital Rock. Interesting remnants of the Indian campground are some pictographs and mortar holes in the flat rocks where the Indians ground acorns for food. Exhibits in a nearby shelter tell the story of these early inhabitants.

The best fishing reached by road in Sequoia National Park is along the Middle Fork of the Kaweah. An easy footpath takes you down from Hospital Rock.

Several scenic turnouts along the route are rewarding stops. Among them Castle Rock, 6½ miles from the entrance station, is a good orientation spot and has a fine view of the spiry Castle Rocks across the canyon. Big Fern and Black Oak Spring are water stops with sparkling springs. Amphitheater Point, 10½ miles into the park, has one of the best overall views of Moro Rock and the Middle Fork's canyon.

TO ATWELL MILL AND MINERAL KING. About 3 miles up the highway from Three Rivers the road to Atwell Mill and Mineral King takes off steeply and winds for more than 20 miles into the High Country.

When you stop for the grand panoramic view from Lookout Point, you've reached an elevation of 4,000 feet. High above the East Fork of the Kaweah River you look southwest across its canyon and up the forested sweep of Case Mountain, outside the park boundary.

More than 2 miles away the individual treetops near the crest are outlined with sunlight. There are the unmistakable rounded crowns of mature sequoias—uncounted, unnamed, and surely in their isolation, safe forever from any complement of little signs telling how big they are.

Atwell Mill, where logging began in 1879, converted hundreds of sequoia trees into lumber. Remains of the old mill can be seen today, and the home of the former operator is beside the road. Among the great stumps in the forest opening, heavy machinery lies rusting in the grass, while young blue-green sequoias dramatically symmetrical and compact, strive to replace their vanished elders. Chunks of the dark wood of felled trees are still lying about, weathered but sound, and the smaller pieces are prime whittling material.

Of special interest is the sequoia found here at an elevation of 8,800 feet, the highest spot at which this species is known to grow. The tree is located north of the road where a trail to the top of Paradise Ridge meanders up through this impressive grove of Big Trees.

There is a small secluded campground and a ranger station at Atwell Mill. If you prefer a place with a comfortable temperature where there aren't many people, this area will appeal to you.

Mineral King, at the end of the road 3 or 4 miles beyond Silver City, was another old mining community. Now it is important as one of the main jumping off spots for trips into Sequoia's High Country and is a controversial site for future development of year-around recreation facilities. Pack stations with horses and burros are located here, and there are several good fishing lakes within a radius of 3 miles. Mineral King lies in a basin and you must climb out to reach the lakes. It is not necessary to go outside the basin to enjoy some fine inspiring one-day walks, easy or strenuous.

Only a few of Mineral King's buildings have withstood the snows, and most of them are now used to provide lodging for wayfarers. There are cabins with rustic housekeeping arrangements like wood stoves, and even one "honeymoon cabin," tucked away in the pines only a few feet from a brook that could provide firm wild trout for breakfast any day. For lodging information and reservations, write to Mineral King Resort, P.O. Box 98, Three Rivers, California 93271.

Giant Forest

The region of the Giant Forest has all of the park's housing accommodations, stores, most of the campgrounds, a visitor center, and the programs, and yet it, too, seems relatively natural. How old-fashioned it is, you may think when you enter Giant Forest Village, and how unhurried—even when summer's crowd overflows the parking space. The stores and the sprinkling of lodge buildings are nostalgic blends of stone, dark boards, and shingles. Giant Forest is 16 miles from Ash Mountain and 30 miles from Grant Grove.

AMONG THE GIANTS. In the Giant Forest are acre upon acre of stately sequoias in nearly pure stands, interrupted in places by sudden meadows, or intermingled with giant pines and firs. At the Village or your camp or lodge you are only on the threshold of the really protected part of Giant Forest's several groves. Just driving in this part of the park will deny you the unforgettable experience that comes from walking through the heart of one of the greatest surviving sequoia forests. At the Lodgepole Visitor Center you can study maps and exhibits, and ask about the best way to use your time on the forest paths.

The General Sherman Tree and its dimensions have been discussed on page 28 of this book, but to really appreciate the tremendous size of the world's largest tree, you must see it, walk around it, and let your eyes follow the massive trunk up and up to the full 272 feet. A ranger naturalist is usually on duty in the summer to talk with you and answer your questions. For a picture without a wide-angle lens on your camera, the closest you can get to an unobstructed view of the huge tree is from a clearing near the parking area.

Near the General Sherman Tree is the start of the Congress Trail, a good 2-mile loop that will take you

OLD MINERAL KING downtown beneath snowy Farewell Gap is beautiful destination or jumping-off place.

MORO ROCK foot path, safe but giddy, leads up bare spine to rock's crest and magnificent view.

The thousands of years of nature's handiwork is explained by a ranger naturalist on daily tours from mid-June to Labor Day, 9 A.M. to 3 P.M. There is a small charge for visitors over 12 years old. It is a good idea to make the earlier tours, as they are less crowded.

A pleasant half-mile path runs beside a musical stream down to the entrance. The trees and shrubs have identification markers, and there are trailside benches.

MORO ROCK is the giant monolith that juts out of the Giant Forest to dominate the wide canyon of the Middle Fork of the Kaweah River. The commanding crest at 6,725 feet looks distant and unattainable from the Generals Highway, but not nearly so forbidding when you get up on the plateau and drive the 2-mile spur road to its northern base. From the parking area there, you climb only 300 feet to the summit. The trail, with safety railings all the way up, follows natural crevices and ledges in some places and otherwise is a carved series of steps and walkways. It is a route full of wide-eyed excitement for most youngsters, and most anyone can make the top. There are plenty of rock seats to rest on.

The reward for continuing on the giddy stone staircase is one of the world's great views. To the west are the low ridges of the Sierra foothills with the flat expanse of the San Joaquin Valley beyond them. The steep walls of the canyons of the Kaweah and its tributaries lie to the south and east, climaxed by the magnificent jagged crest of the Great Western Divide.

Enroute to Moro Rock, on the left side of the road, the Auto Log invites the motorist to take pictures of his car on top of it.

CRESCENT MEADOW. John Muir was so impressed by Crescent Meadow that he referred to it as the "gem of the Sierra." It is a lovely crescent-shaped meadow surrounded by a wall of dark and stately forest trees. A tiny stream runs through it, and youngsters will be delighted with the many small trout always seen toward the lower end. (No fishing, though!) The meadow is boggy, and flowers bloom throughout the summer, especially during the early part when the ground is covered with shooting stars, yellow monkey flowers, and other moisture-loving plants.

A half-mile hike from Crescent Meadow parking area brings you to Tharp's Log. You can go inside the log where pioneer Hale Tharp spent his summers and where John Muir was a guest.

The road to Crescent Meadow branches left from the Moro Rock Road a little less than 2 miles from the Village. It passes under a fallen sequoia called Tunnel Log, which has been cut so that cars can pass under it.

A short distance beyond Tunnel Log is the Mather Plaque, placed as it has been in other national parks as a tribute to Stephen T. Mather, first director of the National Park Service.

About one-tenth of a mile beyond the plaque is the Black Chamber, a sequoia which has refused to die, even

to some of the more famous and spectacular of the trees, including the Senate and House groups and the Founder's Group, as well as the President, the McKinley, and the Chief Sequoyah trees. At the beginning of the trail a guide booklet is available explaining the numbered stakes along the way.

You could stroll the Giant Forest's paths for days without covering the same ground twice. But perhaps the greatest concentration of wonders is in an area composing about one third of the forest that begins with the Congress Trail. You can loop back to your starting point at any of several branches.

Eventually it will not be the size and age of the sequoias that will mean the most to you (not all of them are large or old), but their mystic beauty. Your eyes will grow keen to every seedling, to every growing cinnamon bole down the forest aisle, and to every towering rounded silhouette on the distant ridge; no other tree identifies itself so well or possesses such powers of enchantment.

CRYSTAL CAVE, 9 miles from Giant Forest, is the only one of the known caves in the park that is open to the public. Here the natural pools are beautiful, the delicate formations and crystalline marble on the walls shimmer in the indirect light, and the temperature is a constant 50 degrees. Strangely, this beautiful and interesting cave was not discovered until 28 years after Sequoia became a national park.

though only a small portion of trunk and foliage remains alive to provide nourishment.

OTHER STROLLS AND HIKES. Many miles of foot trails in the Giant Forest area give you an opportunity to take delightful walks from 1 to 2 hours or more in length. One trip of less than a mile takes you along the edge of Sunset campground to Sunset Rock and affords some spectacular views. As its name implies, the rock should be visited at sunset for the best effects. Beetle Rock is similar and is located west of the Village near Camp Kaweah. If at times you forget that there are other worlds besides the human world in which you live, go to Beetle Rock, sit a while and watch the world of insects and birds and lizards and a host of other small animals. An entire book, *A Day On Beetle Rock*, by Sally Carraghar, was written about just this experience.

A walk of about 1½ miles will take you to Huckleberry Meadow with its old squatter's cabin. You can return by a different route or continue on to Crescent Meadow less than half a mile farther.

You can hike from Giant Forest Lodge to Hanging Rock (less than 1½ miles); or if you don't feel particularly ambitious, drive about 1½ miles toward Moro Rock, park near Trinity Corner, and walk the .3 mile to Hanging Rock.

BEARPAW MEADOW. This is a trip of trips from Giant Forest if you want to get an idea of some of the back country of Sequoia and do not have time to explore much of it. Bearpaw is an 11-mile hike, but perhaps an easier day's trip on horseback.

Bearpaw Meadow Camp is perched on the edge of a tremendous overlook at the base of the Great Western Divide. In addition to the spectacular view, the camp has comfort, good food, and good fellowship. Side trails can be taken through fine mountain country to good stream and lake fishing.

The camp is generally open from the last week in June to the first of September. Tent accommodations are about $5.00 per person. You should make reservations at the lodge well in advance of your trip.

The trips to Alta Peak, and to Heather, Emerald, and Pear lakes, which also originate in this area, are described with the High Country adventures on pages 30 and 31.

AT BEARPAW MEADOW CAMP, early morning risers stuff their backpacks with lunches and fishing gear. The High Country camp is located on a breathtaking perch on the shoulder of a deep canyon.

KINGS CANYON, *with Kings River flowing through, is viewed from road that takes you down to the bottom.*

KINGS CANYON NATIONAL PARK

Kings Canyon differs from other national parks in that no road cuts across it; it is necessary to go far to the south or north to get from one side to the other. You should know ahead where your activities will be centered, so you won't find yourself on the opposite side.

This park actually consists of two entirely separate areas. The west side, somewhat separated from the main body of the park, contains the only two developed sections, the General Grant Grove and Kings Canyon regions. It is densely forested and usually comfortably cool (elevation varies from 5,000 to 9,000 feet). The main part of the park, on the other hand, is a rugged mass of spectacular peaks and canyons. This great interior is the High Country discussed on pages 29 through 35.

General Grant Grove Region

Principal claims to fame in this area are three sequoia groves: the Grant, the Redwood Mountain, and what remains of another in the Big Stump area.

GENERAL GRANT GROVE is the destination of most visitors to the area, since it has all the park facilities as well as the famed General Grant Tree. Roads in the grove take you almost to the base of the Grant Tree, to its towering live companions (many named for states), and to its fallen companions, Dead Giant and Fallen Monarch (horses were once stabled in its strong shell). The General Grant Tree is the largest in the park, almost as big as Sequoia's General Sherman and just as popular with visitors. The General Grant Tree is also the Nation's Christmas Tree, and each Yule Season an impressive ceremony is held there.

Near the Grant Tree, the Centennial Stump, a striking contrast to the living giant, is all that remains of the great tree cut for the 1875 Philadelphia World's Fair and reassembled for the amazement of easterners.

Grant Grove Village is beside a big meadow a mile from the General Grant Tree. Here there is a visitor center, most service facilities, and accommodations, some on pine-forested slopes.

Campfire programs every summer night at the amphitheater deal with different aspects of the park—its flora and fauna, or its high country, or the history of the early-day cutting of the giants. At many places in the Village you will find posted schedules of daily trips full of facts and lore, conducted by a ranger naturalist. Most are 1 or 2 hour walks starting about 9 A.M. There are 6-hour trips each week, for which you bring your lunch and walk about 5 miles. The park programs along with pamphlets available at the Village can educate you well on the sequoias.

If you just want to contemplate the wonder of it all, you can go to the landmark trees and groves on your own. A wonderful labyrinth of trails radiates from Grant

CHARMING IN ITS SECLUSION, *Redwood Canyon on Redwood Creek is away from the mainstream of visitors; you enjoy quiet walks through stands of inspiring giant sequoias and their fallen companions.*

Grove Village. Within an area of 5 square miles, there are over 20 miles of trails, most of them comparatively level where you can wander leisurely under the giants away from the sounds of civilization.

Panoramic Point is reached by the road that turns right less than half a mile beyond the Village. A short walk from the parking area takes you to a sweeping view across the deep canyons of the Kings River to the high peaks beyond.

REDWOOD MOUNTAIN GROVE usually refers to the 10,000 acres of Redwood Mountain and Redwood Canyon, the largest remaining concentration of giant sequoias in the world. This huge valley and mountain ridge of sequoias is off the beaten track and many people miss it; solitude adds to its charm. On the canyon floor or on the slopes of the mountain you can walk through pure stands of giant sequoias.

Two of the guided walks from Grant Grove, Sugar Bowl and Barton's Post Camp, go into Redwood Mountain Grove. In Sugar Bowl itself, you can stand in one spot and count 57 lofty sequoias. It has the cathedral quality of the more famous sequoia groves, but without the constant flow of people. From either point, hikers can continue on an all-day loop that takes them through more redwoods and patches of manzanita, along pretty streams with waterfalls to the Hart Tree, the world's

fourth largest. It is 10 feet higher than the Grant, but it has a smaller perimeter—73 feet.

The starting place for all walks in Redwood Mountain Grove is a parking lot at the foot of a dirt road that drops down into the canyon from Generals Highway. You turn onto it 5 miles south of Grant Grove Village.

Redwood Mountain Overlook, a turnoff viewing point on this stretch of highway looks down into Redwood Canyon and out along the spine of Redwood Mountain. This is a good way for anyone who is going to hike in this area to get the lay of the land.

BIG STUMP GROVE, a short and easy walk from the Big Stump entrance station, contains Sawed Tree, Mark Twain Stump, and Old Adam or Burnt Monarch (a huge, burned out, hollow stump that, when intact, may have been the greatest of all the giant sequoias). Down the hill to the northwest from Mark Twain Stump and Old Adam is most of Big Stump Basin, an 800-acre area that was completely logged off in the 1880's and now has many slender young sequoia seedlings.

See it not for what is there now, but for what it might have been had it not been lumbered. Some sequoia stumps exhibit more than 3,000 annual growth rings. Here is an indelible lesson in conservation which illustrates clearly how man can destroy in a few hours something that took nature thousands of years to build.

CLOUD CANYON *and Cement Table camp on up-stream Roaring River is reached on trail to Colby Pass.*

EVOLUTION BASIN *traveler on Muir Trail stops at Sapphire Lake, Mt. Huxley before reaching Muir Pass.*

Kings Canyon and Cedar Grove Region

From Grant Grove you go to Kings Canyon and Cedar Grove on a 30-mile highway that drops 2,000 feet before reaching its destination. From parking overlooks on wide sweeping curves, you can look into the canyons of Middle and South forks of the Kings River and beyond to the bewildering maze of jagged peaks which constitute the greater portion of Kings Canyon National Park. These breathtaking views are the best hints you will get of the "country beyond."

Where the road crosses the river 10 miles before Cedar Grove, you will see the parking area and buildings at Boyden Cave. The entire trip through the privately owned cave, including the 10-minute walk from the parking area, takes only an hour. Most of the time you will be from 450 to 600 feet underground. The trail is well lighted and equipped with hand rails. Guided tours, from 11 A.M. to 4 P.M. daily have a nominal admission charge.

For the last 10 miles to Cedar Grove, the road follows the South Fork—a Jekyll-Hyde sort of stream which at high water becomes a roaring torrent full of trees and

brush and with a frightening power that has, in the past, demolished the road. During mid and late summer when the waters are low, the river still rushes, but with a musical sound, and a good fisherman can find sport in the pools and rapids.

Cedar Grove has a store, coffee shop, ranger station, and a few cabins. A variety of conducted trips led by ranger naturalists are offered here, as well as nightly illustrated campfire programs.

Summer days can be warm at this elevation of 4,600 feet, yet camping is delightful under the big pines on the bank of the boisterous river.

An easy walk of about 3 miles leaves the Roaring River Falls parking area (3 miles beyond the store) and takes the trail up to Zumwalt Meadows. Just below the meadows, a foot bridge crosses the river, enabling you to return to your car on the road. If you feel energetic or are getting in shape for a high country trip, keep on past Zumwalt Meadows to the Bubbs Creek Bridge (about 4½ miles), across the creek, and back down on the other side. Another good trip of about 5 miles each way is from the parking area at Copper Creek up the river to Mist Falls and return. The trail is comparatively level except for the last half mile, and that is not bad.

At Roads End at Copper Creek is a long-term parking area where you can leave your car for a week or a month while you are in the back country. If you have some free time, go up to the end of the road and watch the picturesque procession heading into the mountains—backpackers, long strings of pack animals, horseback riders, and men, women, and children leading burros, all pass this way from Cedar Grove.

The National Park Service has committed itself never to extend the road beyond Copper Creek, its present terminus; so this is literally "the end of civilization." Beyond is the wilderness of Kings Canyon National Park, the finest the High Sierra has to offer. Beyond is High Adventure.

SEQUOIA IN WINTER

For the winter sports enthusiast or for one who simply enjoys sitting before a fire and watching it snow on the other side of the window, Sequoia National Park in winter has a great deal to offer. You can enjoy the snow actively or passively.

It can be delightful to drive slowly through a snowy forest, hearing no sound except the crunching of spotless snow under your tires. A road made to order for contemplation of a Western winter is the Generals Highway. Except for brief closings during and after storms it is kept open all winter, but bring your chains and check an automobile club for conditions before coming. Between General Grant Grove and Giant Forest, the Generals Highway passes through sublime forest scenery, where giant sequoias with their cinnamon-red trunks stand in warm contrast to the cool blue shadows and white highlights of the snow. Spend some of your time out of your car looking up at the huge trees in their winter dress. You can safely take walks close to the road in Giant Forest; and north of Giant Forest Village, you can walk out into Round Meadow encircled by Big Trees. Snowshoes, if you need them, can be rented at Giant Forest.

Winter Sports

If your trip is to include winter sports, Sequoia has two popular areas of recreation; and snow equipment from skis to skates to snowshoes can be rented. A mile beyond the General Sherman Tree in Giant Forest, you can take a side road to the Wolverton ski area. Slopes agreeable to different degrees of skill are reached by three rope tows.

Accomplished ski-tourers can start at Wolverton for the 6-mile ascent east through Panther Meadow to the Pear Lake Hut, where there is overnight shelter but no supplies. The return trip is a swooping thriller that compensates for the 2,000-foot climb. Register at a ranger station (Giant Forest or Lodgepole) before you go.

There are no prepared toboggan runs at Wolverton, but there are slopes for sledding and sliding.

To ice skate at the open-air skating rink at Lodgepole, one of the few such rinks in the Western mountains, turn off the highway a mile beyond the Wolverton road.

If you find the land of the Big Trees beautiful in summer, you will find them so in a different way in winter. The air is crisp, the stars in the winter sky seem especially large, and a stillness settles over Giant Forest—a stillness in strange contrast to the bustle of summer. Again, you don't have to be a sportsman to get out into and enjoy this winterland. Put on your warm clothes and walk along the road some evening after dinner. You will find a new beauty and appreciation in the silence of the sequoias in winter.

SNOW ON SEQUOIAS *accentuates great size, creates a stillness as you walk through them in winter.*

LASSEN VOLCANIC NATIONAL PARK

History of a recent volcano recorded on a once-peaceful land

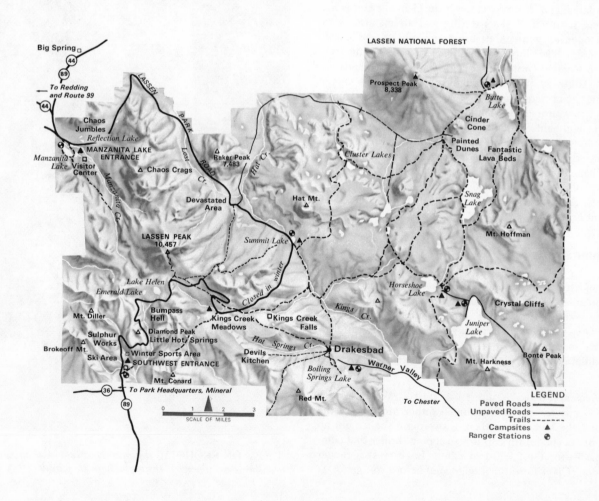

LASSEN NATIONAL FOREST

Big Spring
44
89
To Redding
and Route 99
44

Chaos
Jumbles
Reflection Lake
MANZANITA LAKE
ENTRANCE
*Manzanita
Lake* Visitor
Center

LASSEN PARK ROAD
Lost Cr.
Manzanita Cr.

△ Chaos Crags

Raker Peak
7,483
Hat Cr.

Devastated
Area

LASSEN PEAK
10,457

Summit Lake

Hat Mt.

Cluster Lakes

Prospect Peak
8,338

Butte
Lake

Cinder
Cone

Painted
Dunes   Fantastic
Lava Beds

*Snag
Lake*

Mt. Hoffman

Lake Helen
Emerald Lake

Closed in winter

Bumpass
Hell

Mt. Diller △

△ Diamond Peak
Little Hot Springs

Kings Creek
Meadows

□ Kings Creek
Falls

Kings   Cr.

*Horseshoe
Lake*

Crystal Cliffs

*Juniper
Lake*

Sulphur
Works
Brokeoff Mt. △   Ski Area
Winter Sports Area
△ SOUTHWEST ENTRANCE

Devils
Kitchen

Hot   Springs   Cr.

Drakesbad

*Boiling
Springs Lake*

Warner   Valley

Mt. Harkness △

Bonte Peak

△ Mt. Conard

36
To Park Headquarters, Mineral

Red Mt.

To Chester

89

0   1   2   3
SCALE OF MILES

LEGEND
Paved Roads ———
Unpaved Roads ------
Trails - - - - -
Campsites ▲
Ranger Stations ⊛

VAPORS RISE *from Boiling Springs Lake (125°).*
transparent to varicolored bottom. Near Drakesbad.

BUMPASS HELL BASIN *is hissing, steaming, bubbling evidence of volcanic activity in Lassen. Hikers*
follow the self-guiding trail through this largest thermal area in the park.

LASSEN IS A BEAUTIFUL and intriguing land of contrasts. Formed by violent volcanic activity, now it is being softened by time and the charm of living things.

Lassen is a park by virtue of the eruptions of Lassen Peak, which has the distinction of being the most recently active volcano in the United States, exclusive of those in Alaska and Hawaii. As a result, Lassen has hot springs and pools, steam vents and fumaroles, mud pots and cinder cones, as well as large denuded expanses of land.

But there is much more. Isolated lakes and singing streams offer good fishing. Beautiful trails lead to out-of-the-way places, over mountain meadows lush with wildflowers in late spring and through dense coniferous forests and friendly groves of quaking aspen with their shimmering green leaves.

Each season at Lassen has its charms; but autumn, from Labor Day to the end of October, is especially delightful—Indian summer with deep blue skies, golden brown and red leaves, pleasantly warm days and crisp nights. Fishing improves from the first of September on, and few people are in the park.

Lassen Volcanic National Park is small enough to give you a feeling of intimacy, large enough to give you freedom on foot or horseback, and different enough to pique the curiosity of even the blasé visitor. The tempo of summer activity at Lassen seems more leisurely than in many parks—away from the pressures of crowds, people take things easier.

This is an area of charming diversification, both in natural features and activities. Whatever it is you are looking for—hiking, riding, swimming, fishing, skiing, scenery, or just relaxation—whether you are camping or staying in the lodges, you'll enjoy the friendly, intimate feeling emitted by this unique national park.

How to Get There

Lassen Volcanic park covers 165 square miles along the southern Cascade Range in Northern California.

BY CAR: There are five ways to enter the park. The northeast corner is reached by a road branching from State Highway 44 and leading to Butte Lake. From the south, the road leaves State 36 at Chester, then forks to go to Drakesbad and Juniper Lake. The Southwest Entrance (State 89) and the Manzanita Lake Entrance on the northwest (State highways 44 and 89) are connected by the main Lassen Park road. These two approaches are reached by Interstate 5; turn off at Redding or Red Bluff.

BY BUS, RAIL AND AIR: Redding, Red Bluff, and Susanville are served by commercial bus lines. Connecting transportation by the concessioner is available to Manzanita Lake from Redding. From Red Bluff and Susanville, commercial buses run to Mineral where concessioner transportation is again available, by reservation, to Manzanita Lake.

Southern Pacific Railroad serves Redding. Western Pacific Railroad stops at Keddie. From June 10 to September 20, concessioner buses will meet trains at Redding, upon prior arrangement.

The nearest commercial airports are at Redding and Red Bluff. During the summer season, concessioner buses will meet planes if previously notified. Light planes can land at Chester, 17 miles southeast of Drakesbad.

Arrange transportation through Lassen National Park Co., Manzanita Lake, California 96060.

Where to Stay

The only accommodations within the park are at Manzanita Lake in the northwest corner, and Drakesbad in the southern part of the park, reached by a secondary road from Chester.

MANZANITA LAKE LODGE, easily accessible, well equipped, and comfortable, is open June 10 to September 20. The main rustic building contains a lobby, curio section, cocktail lounge, and a dining room where meals are attractively served and reasonably priced.

The Lodge has a variety of cabins and cottages, priced from $10.00 for one, and from $11.00 for two. Most luxurious are the hotel bungalow bedrooms. For a family wishing housekeeping accommodations, the Pine Cottages offer excellent facilities, including all kitchen utensils, for $18.50 to $26.00 a day. Lower-priced housekeeping cabins are also available.

DRAKESBAD GUEST RANCH is the place to go if you wish solitude and more rustic surroundings. Accommodations here are limited to fifty. The main building contains hotel rooms. There are also modern furnished cottages. Advance reservations are needed.

Drakesbad Guest Ranch usually opens later and closes a few days earlier than Manzanita Lake Lodge. A room for two begins at $28.00 including three meals and swimming. Children have special rates when sharing rooms.

There are horses and guides here for pack trips and trail rides. For the angler, several lakes and streams with excellent fishing are easily accessible. This is the gateway to the Lassen Wilderness.

CAMPGROUNDS. There are eight campgrounds well distributed throughout the park. Some have modern conveniences, while others are rustic and undeveloped.

You will find four campgrounds along the Lassen Park Road—Manzanita Lake, Summit Lake, Kings Creek, and Sulphur Works, which is a walk-in camp.

The large Manzanita Lake Campground has the longest season, usually from the first of May to mid-October; is within walking distance of a store and post office; and is well patronized.

Summit Lake has swimming, boating, and fishing. If your primary interest is hiking or riding, this is the

QUIESCENT LASSEN PEAK *looms above the scene of its devastating eruption of 1915, which left trees lying away from the lava flow. Northeast side is now undergoing natural reforestation.*

place to stay. Many of the park trails begin in this area, and stables are nearby where riding and pack animals can be rented.

Kings Creek is a beautiful, primitive campground with only 18 campsites. Because it is the highest in the park (7,150 feet), it is cool and has a short season. You shouldn't plan to camp here before mid-July or after Labor Day.

Of the remaining four campgrounds, Butte Lake is rather isolated, but restful and popular for its good fishing and proximity to Cinder Cone. It has boat rentals and a ranger station. To reach it, drive 11 miles from Old Station on State 44, then follow the 6-mile dirt road leading south.

Warner Valley Campground is on the road to Drakesbad. It offers stream fishing and is within easy hiking distance of the thermal areas of Boiling Springs Lake, Thermal Geyser (not a true geyser), and Devil's Kitchen. As the road is rugged and steep, only small trailers are advised.

Juniper Lake Campground, about 16 miles from Chester, has fishing and several good hiking trails. One trail leads to the top of Mt. Harkness with its fire lookout. The campground is small, and it is necessary to use the lake water, which should be boiled first.

Less than 2 miles beyond Juniper is Horseshoe Lake Campground. Here, water comes from springs and need not be boiled, and the fishing is better.

All campgrounds in the park have a 14-day limit. Manzanita Lake, Summit Lake, and Butte Lake have spaces for trailers, but no hookup for electricity, water, or sewage. These three also have campfire programs.

Special campgrounds are set aside for organized groups up to 200 persons. Advance reservations must be made through the park superintendent.

HISTORY

There is no record of the first pioneer to see the hot pools and steaming valleys of Lassen. We can only surmise that it was someone from an emigrant party that moved into Northern California during the late 1840's or early 1850's.

Lassen Peak itself was named for Peter Lassen, a Danish immigrant and early pioneer in the region who conducted parties from Humboldt, Nevada into the Sacramento Valley for a few years beginning in 1848. Legend has it Lassen was not too skilled a guide, that he frequently became lost himself, and that the so-called

SMOKE COLUMN from 1915 eruption climbed 5 miles into the sky and was visible for 50 miles; 5-ton rocks were catapulted into the air. Touring party watches from a discreet distance.

Lassen Trail, which passed within 6 miles of the present park area, was anything but a direct route. Some historians suggest that Peter used Lassen Peak (then called St. Joseph's Mountain) for a landmark one day, Mount Shasta the next, and never knew the difference. Legend also relates that once when Lassen became lost, the group he was guiding forced him at gunpoint to climb the peak which now bears his name in order to get his correct location.

By 1850, well-founded rumors circulated the uncertainties and hazards of the Lassen Trail. Fewer and fewer travelers elected to use it, and Northern California settlements began to suffer.

Promotion methods being much the same in those days, the businessmen of these settlements, to lure the emigrants, had a new route laid out which was admittedly much better and shorter than the Lassen Trail. Known as the Nobles Trail, this new route ran between Black Rock, Nevada, and Fort Reading, California (now Redding). It entered what is now Lassen Park at Butte Lake, traversed the northern section of the present park, and left it near Manzanita Lake. Nobles Trail proved popular from the beginning and was used for many years. Although overgrown in places with chaparral, the old trail is still visible today.

Lassen Peak and Cinder Cone National Monument was established in 1907. The eruptions of Lassen Peak beginning in 1914 subsequently led to the establishment of the national park in 1916.

The Story of a Volcano

Fiery explosions, flows of lava, and slow-moving glaciers —this is the history of Lassen Volcanic National Park. Once completely covered by water, the landscape now reveals a 12-million-year history of eruptions. The Cascade Range is volcanic in origin, and such well known peaks as Baker, Rainier, Adams, Hood, Shasta, and Lassen are all old volcanoes of which Lassen is the most recently active. Lassen is also the southernmost of the major Cascade peaks that poured forth their lavas and formed a link in the great Pacific Circle of Fire—a chain of volcanoes which ring the Pacific Ocean.

Lassen Peak itself is the offspring of a much greater volcano—Mount Tehama, which was 11,000 feet high (over a thousand feet higher than Lassen) and measured 15 miles across its base. The ancestral Mount Tehama eventually collapsed, probably for lack of support. Then 5 to 6 thousand years ago, Lassen Peak pushed its way into existence on the northern slope of Mount Tehama's remnants. If you have an eye for geological landscapes, you will recognize its fractured remnants nearby—Brokeoff Mountain, Mount Diller, Pilot Pinnacle, Mount Conrad, and Diamond Point.

THE INDIANS

During your Lassen visit, you can see Indian exhibits in the visitor center and museum at Manzanita Lake and attend the Indian Lore Program given twice daily. Here you learn much of the history, habits, and customs of the Indians in this area of northeastern California.

No battles were fought, no emigrant trains were attacked and burned, no settlers were murdered here. The park area was a summer camping, hunting, and fishing place for the Atsugewi, Yana, Yahi, and Mountain Maidu. They came in the spring, following the deer to higher elevations, and remained until late fall when they returned to their permanent homes in the valleys and foothills. All four tribes lived near one another in a fairly peaceful manner and occasionally even intermarried.

Their habits and customs were similar—that of simple, peace-loving hill and mountain people. Combined, the four tribes had a population of perhaps 4,025 in 1770, but by 1950 this number had dwindled to 385. A few of their descendants, about 70, still live in the vicinity of Lassen.

The life, beliefs, and customs of these early people are interesting, and their history contains a fascinating tale—the story of Ishi, the last survivor of the Yahi Tribe.

In 1908, it was estimated that only five members of the Yahi Tribe remained. In a completely wild state, they had been seen only once. Then, in 1916, a half-starved, emaciated creature speaking in a tongue no one had ever heard and wearing nothing but a torn piece of canvas over his shoulders was "captured" near a slaughter house in the vicinity of Oroville. He called himself Ishi, "I am a man." In spite of his condition, Ishi refused food and remained huddled in the corner of a cell where a sheriff had locked him. Here he might have died had not word reached the Department of Anthropology at the University of California about "The Wild Man of Oroville." Excitedly following a hunch, anthropologist, Dr. Alfred L. Kroeber left posthaste for Oroville. If his hunch were correct, the "wild man" was the most remarkable anthropological discovery in years—the lone living representative of a little known people thought to be extinct.

The professor's job, difficult at best, was further complicated because no one knew the Yahi language.

BASKET-MAKING techniques, demonstrated by local Indian woman, are feature of park's naturalist program.

His only aid was a list of words from the vocabulary of a people known to be the closest relatives of the Yahi. Patiently, he went through the list and finally he hit a word that brought a delighted response from Ishi. From this beginning the professor gained the Indian's confidence and was finally able to take him to Berkeley.

Ishi died of tuberculosis five years later, but during that period he made many friends among the museum staff and contributed knowledge about a people of which he was the last survivor. You will find the detailed story of Ishi in the widely acclaimed book *Ishi In Two Worlds*, by Theodora Kroeber, Dr. Kroeber's widow, published in 1961.

The first settlers of this area assumed that Lassen Peak volcano was extinct, though the earth around it was pockmarked with bubbling sinks. But on May 30, 1914, a great column of steam and gases spouted from the peak, throwing out lava and debris on the upper slopes. The brief eruption opened a new vent in the crater and marked the beginning of a year of activity. Lassen erupted 150 times, spouting dust and steam high in the air and flinging cinders and small boulders around its base. No lava flowed, however, and spectators were more curious than concerned.

Then on May 19, 1915, molten lava bubbled up to the crater rim and spilled over the sides, melting snow and sending 20-ton boulders and a devastating mudflow down the valleys of Hat Creek and Lost Creek on the northeastern slope.

Three days later Lassen Peak again exploded into violence. A spectacular column of vapor and ash rose over 5 miles in the air. So powerful was the eruption that ashes drifted over Reno, Nevada, where the streets were covered with several inches of powdery debris. At the same time, a terrifying blast of steam and hot gas roared down the northeastern slope, killing every living thing in its path, knocking trees down like matchsticks, and scrubbing the earth bare.

With this cataclysmic release, Lassen's activity slowly declined. Some minor eruptions continued through the

BEAUTIFULLY SYMMETRICAL Cinder Cone is a true volcano, which erupted in 1851 with such violence that the lava cooled in the air and dropped in an even fall of cinders that piled 700 feet high.

year, but by 1917 most visible activity had subsided. Today you can see the results of the blast in the Devastated Area. All felled trees point away from the peak. At the top, you can explore the craters, which have long since cooled. However, below the surface, the volcanic pot still boils. Where the earth's crust is broken or cracked, gases and steam still hiss through fumaroles.

Another evidence of pent-up forces beneath the earth is Cinder Cone, a recently formed volcano that rises 700 feet near Butte Lake. An eruption of Cinder Cone was reported by an emigrant party in 1851.

Lassen Volcanic National Park abounds with evidence of dying volcanic activity. Hot springs, steam vents, and fumaroles still persist, many years after eruptions have subsided. The most accessible is Sulphur Works, on the road a short distance inside the Southwest Entrance. About 5 miles farther is the trail which leads through Bumpass Hell, the largest and best known thermal area in the park. Steam also rises from Little Hot Springs Valley as you drive over the main road. A thermal area in Warner Valley is within easy walking distance of Drakesbad. Here, a trail leads you to Boiling Springs Lake. Turbulent Terminal Geyser and Devil's Kitchen are also nearby.

A word of caution—watch your step, keep on the trails, and don't go near the edge of hot pools. The crust is thin in places and severe burns have resulted from people being too enthusiastic and too venturesome.

Two questions frequently asked about the park are: "Why are there hot springs?" and "Will the peak ever erupt again?" Hot springs occur where hot magma and rock is sufficiently near the surface to heat rain and snow water seepage. The second inquiry is difficult to answer. After all, the eruption of the beautiful, quiescent peak was not expected some 50 years ago. If it were to erupt again, however, it would probably give advance warning.

PLANTS AND ANIMALS

Frequent eruptions repeatedly destroyed plants and wildlife in Lassen, but life has repeatedly returned and today it is abundant.

At lower elevations you will find white fir and a host of pines—Jeffrey, ponderosa, lodgepole, western white, and sugar pine. Near Manzanita Lake grows some incense cedar and Douglas-fir; and higher up, red fir and mountain hemlock. Still higher, near timberline, are white bark pines, their trunks often gnarled and twisted by the force of the wind. Cottonwood, alder, willow, and aspen are all part of the scene, especially where the land is moist. Part of the charm of Lassen's streams is the cool shade and the dancing sunlight and shadow contributed by these trees.

Chaparral covers many hillsides of Lassen, composed mainly of snowbrush ceanothus, chinquapin, and manzanita. Around Manzanita Lake, great treeless hillsides are covered with dense thickets of greenleaf manzanita, unmistakable for its leathery green leaves, red bark, and in spring, masses of small bright pink flowers.

Wildflowers are everywhere in Lassen, from water-loving ladies-thumb in lakes to drought-resistant lupine on dry lava flows.

When spring arrives, you will find Indian paint brush, bleeding heart, monkey flowers, leopard lily, and a host of other blooms. Many persist throughout the summer. In the higher mountain meadows, mountain-heath, lupine, and penstemon put on their finest display in August.

The showy red snow plant is abundant. You'll also see orange wallflower, bog Kalmia, balsam root, monkshood, shooting stars, dainty white rein orchid, and the blue forget-me-not or sticksee. There are several hundred flower species in the park, all adding charm and color to the landscape.

You'll see one animal in Lassen that is rare in other California national parks—the Columbia blacktailed deer. The familiar mule deer is also here, though he is less common. Black bears in Lassen seem to have good manners, yet are few in number and seldom seen.

Ground squirrels and chipmunks are numerous. Pine squirrels, or chickarees, chatter from the trees; and in the wooded sections a distance away from the roads, you may be lucky enough to spot a pine marten. Sometimes in the meadows, you may be able to catch a glimpse of the Cascade red foxes that are common here. Marmots, or woodchucks, are occasionally seen, usually at higher elevations.

About 160 species of birds have been identified in this park, from hummingbirds to bald eagles. Lassen, with its abundant vegetation, meadows, lakes and streams, is an ideal place for bird study, especially in fall when lakes are alive with waterfowl. Some water-loving species such as killdeer, belted kingfisher, and water ouzel are here most of the year.

EXPLORING LASSEN

Lassen Volcanic National Park is a beautiful and refreshing nature park, offering visitors most of its scenic and recreational attractions with very easy access. Many of the park's attractions are near the main road, and more than 150 miles of trail lead into the fresh and sparkling land of Lassen.

The booklet *Road Guide to Lassen Volcanic National Park* is keyed to numbered stakes at attractions along Lassen Park Road and will help you enjoy them all. The handy booklet can be purchased at entrance stations or contact stations.

A museum is located at Manzanita Lake, where many interpretive programs are presented. Naturalist programs, held at various points throughout the park, tell

SERENE CONTRAST to the land of the volcano is beauty of Shadow Lake and others, good for trout fishing.

BEAUTIFUL MANZANITA LAKE reflects Lassen Peak, is a favorite visitor area and photography subject.

MOONSCAPE TERRAIN of Chaos Jumbles is result of pink lava rockslides riding on slippery base of wet volcanic ash across level ground and even uphill from Chaos Crags. It covers 2 square miles.

the Lassen story of geology, plants, animals, and history. Park naturalists lead nature walks and hikes to points of interest. Campfire talks are featured at Manzanita Lake, Summit Lake, and Butte Lake campgrounds. Self-guiding nature trails to Cinder Cone, Bumpass Hell, Lassen Peak, Lily Pond, and Boiling Springs Lake have accompanying leaflets detailing natural history features along the way. The museum has more information for this varied naturalist program.

You'll find that the sparkling fishing lakes and volcanic peaks are included with thermal areas as special attractions of this park. Below are a few of the places you will want to see while at Lassen.

MANZANITA AND REFLECTION LAKES are on either side of the highway just inside the northwestern boundary. Here is good fishing, boating, and swimming. (No boating is allowed on Reflection Lake.) If you're a photographer, you can snap some spectacular color pictures of Lassen Peak with Manzanita Lake in the foreground. The scene is especially beautiful when the first snows have touched the peak and the foliage has turned to blazing fall colors.

At Manzanita Lake, the main gathering spot of the park, the Loomis Museum has outstanding exhibits, including a diorama showing Lassen Peak before and after the eruption. Near the museum is a seismograph, that records earth tremors with delicate instruments which may be viewed through a window.

Lily Pond Trail is a fine self-guiding nature trail that circles part of Reflection Lake. This easy stroll of less

than an hour is pleasant and instructive as well.

BUMPASS HELL by its name is a warning, so called for a Lassen pioneer who had the misfortune to plunge a leg into one of the hot springs while showing the area to a visiting newsman.

Bumpass Hell is the largest and showiest of thermal areas in Lassen. Here you'll find a 10-acre basin dissolved out of hard lava by hot acids. You'll see violently roaring hot springs, boiling muddy pools, crystallined sulfur vents, gurgling mud volcanoes, deep turquoise waters over layers of fool's gold, and a mineralized hot stream. In the chill air of morning, hot vapors that issue from thermal springs condense into showy white clouds and hang languidly above hissing fumaroles and wheezing solfataras.

The self-guiding trail to Bumpass Hell begins near Emerald Lake, about 7 miles along the Lassen Park Road from the Southwest Entrance. Remember to stay on trails in the thermal areas.

Sulphur Works, the first hot springs area you reach from the Southwest Entrance, is the most accessible one and is explored on a self-guiding trail.

CINDER CONE is less than 2 miles from Butte Lake in the northeastern corner of the park. Access to both is by a road that turns south off State 44. The volcanic cone was formed by explosive eruptions which ejected volcanic ash and cinder from a central vent, building the symmetrical cone. A trail from Butte Lake to Cinder Cone winds along the edge of the fantastic lava beds that were laid down in part during the 1851 eruption. If you take this trail, be sure to go the one-half mile to the top of the cone. Though the porous cinders readily absorb the heaviest rainfall without altering the cone, they will retain the marks of footprints indefinitely. You can explore the crater, and the 700-foot height affords a fine view of surrounding lava flows.

LASSEN PEAK can be conquered easily by the average hiker. The trail is good and only 2.2 miles long. You climb 2,000 feet in elevation from the highway to the summit. Four hours is ample time for the round trip. At the summit are several small steam vents and in early summer, a sapphire crater pool.

From the highest point, you will see dramatic evidence of Lassen's recent volcanic activity. Also in view are the distant peaks of the Sierra near Lake Tahoe, the Coast Range as it ascends northward to the Trinity Alps, and 75 airline miles away the icy cone of Mount Shasta.

Northeast of the peak, the main park road crosses the area devastated in the 1915 eruption, now undergoing natural reforestation. Farther north are the rugged Chaos Crags, hardened pink plugs of thick, pasty lava undercut by steam explosions that caused the rockslides of Chaos Jumbles. The park highway passes through this debris near Manzanita Lake.

THE DRAKESBAD AREA has a number of interesting thermal features reached by short walks from the Drakesbad resort. You can pick up one of the leaflets there to follow the 2-mile trail around Boiling Springs Lake. This trail first crosses a beautiful meadow and ascends gradually through a deep forest of lodgepole pine, red and white fir. It also leads through an area where trees were killed recently by an extension of thermal activity. Boiling Springs Lake itself boils and bubbles with the action of subsurface springs and steam vents, and the land around it roars and hisses with jets of escaping steam and bubbles with large mud pots.

SNAG LAKE has an unusual appearance. The lake level has risen in recent years, isolating pines and clumps of willows off the south shore. A lava flow, only 100 years old and still unsoftened by nature, forms the north shore, giving the lake a look of other-worldly desolation. You may see water birds such as ducks and gulls, and perhaps the blue heron.

You reach Snag Lake from Horseshoe Lake by one of the park's most beautiful trails. Much of it follows Grassy Creek through meadows. This creek is a spawning place for Snag Lake Trout. Horseshoe Lake, reached by the road from Chester, is also the beginning of a marked trail to the primitive Twin Lakes Wilderness.

SUBWAY CAVE LAVA TUBE, outside the park in Lassen National Forest, is well worth seeing. It is located about 15 miles north of the Manzanita Lake Entrance via State 89. The tube is a long tunnel formed in one of the big lava flows. The outside of the flow cooled and consolidated while the core was still liquid. When the core drained, a lava shell was left through which you can walk.

About halfway between the park and the Lava Tube is Big Spring where you can stop and watch torrents of water gushing from the ground. The flow from this spring is estimated at around 300 gallons each minute.

LASSEN IN WINTER

Lassen is snow country. The snowfall is so heavy, sometimes 50 feet in a season, that the Lassen Park Road is closed by the end of October and often not reopened until June. Even then you will drive through snow canyons that reach far above your car. However, the park is open all year and as you might suspect, skiing is good until early summer.

The Lassen Park Ski Area, located just inside the Southwest Entrance, is not large, but does attract many weekend skiers. The resort can accommodate all kinds of skiers with beginner and intermediate tows, a poma lift, and excellent terrain and snow conditions for cross-country skiing. Ski rental equipment is available; and breakfast, lunch, and light refreshments are sold at the snack bar in the Lassen Chalet.

Ice skating is often good in December on Reflection Lake. The road in this area is kept open from the northwest entrance to the visitor center at Manzanita Lake.

There are no accommodations open in the park during the winter months, but overnight facilities are available at Mineral and several small resorts along State highways 36 and 89 on southern approaches to the park.

WINTER WORLD and Bumpass Hell transform each other into rare sight, reached only by skis or snowshoes.

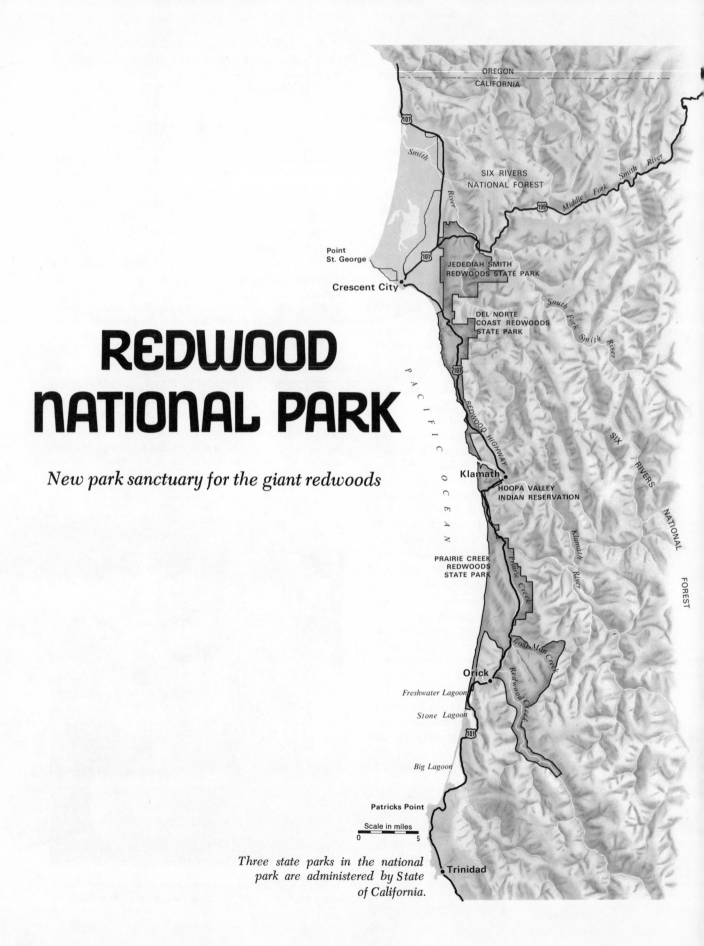

REDWOOD NATIONAL PARK

New park sanctuary for the giant redwoods

OREGON

CALIFORNIA

101

Smith

SIX RIVERS
NATIONAL FOREST

River

199

Middle Fork *Smith River*

Point
St. George

JEDEDIAH SMITH
REDWOODS STATE PARK

South Fork Smith River

Crescent City

DEL NORTE
COAST REDWOODS
STATE PARK

P
A
C
I
F
I
C

O
C
E
A
N

101

REDWOOD HIGHWAY

SIX
RIVERS

NATIONAL

Klamath

HOOPA VALLEY
INDIAN RESERVATION

Klamath River

FOREST

PRAIRIE CREEK
REDWOODS
STATE PARK

Prairie Creek

Lost Man Creek

Orick

Redwood Creek

Freshwater Lagoon

Stone Lagoon

101

Big Lagoon

Patricks Point

Scale in miles
0   5

*Three state parks in the national
park are administered by State
of California.*

Trinidad

REDWOOD FOREST *of revered "old growth" trees is typified by fine stand on Little Lost Man Creek.*

ROAMING HERD OF ROOSEVELT ELK *is seen on beach at the mouth of unnamed creek. Two herds of the wild animals, native to park area, are found along Gold Bluffs Beach and in prairie.*

THE REDWOOD NATIONAL PARK, stretching for 55 coastal miles in the extreme northern part of California, became the state's newest preserve in the national park system shortly before this book went to press. The bill establishing the park was signed by President Johnson on October 2, 1968, climaxing a long-standing and complex controversy. For nearly a century, conservation-minded individuals and groups have worked to preserve the finest remaining specimens of coast redwoods, some of which were growing before the time of Christ; and over the years some protected areas were set up as a result of their efforts. These include such areas as Valley of the Giants, Big Basin Redwoods State Park, and Muir Woods National Monument (donated by a California congressman), all established early in the movement. But the establishment of a national park, a major step in saving the redwoods in their natural surroundings and bringing their value and unique qualities to the attention of the American people, had not been realized until now.

Redwood National Park (an unofficial name at this time) is a beach and forest land containing a great variety of natural features, plant life, and wildlife. The landscape ranges from rocky or sandy beaches and lagoon-marked coastline, inland to bluffs and headlands, and then to the rugged land of high ridges and deep river-cut valleys.

The coast redwoods (*Sequoia sempervirens*) are among the tallest and oldest of living things. They have been known to grow to over 450 feet, and have been reported up to 2,200 years old. The only place that these venerable giants grow in their natural habitat in the world today is within the narrow band of land (about 25 miles wide at the most) along 500 miles of California coast from the San Luis Obispo-Monterey county line to just over the northern border into Oregon.

The major attributes of the redwood trees are their size and age. In *A Natural History of Western Trees*, Donald Culross Peattie calls them a titan race, "... not just occasionally taller, ... but taller as a whole, as a race. ..." The fact that these trees have been able to live so long and reach such great height is due to other unique qualities that give them resistance to fire, pests, and disease.

The redwood forests themselves are among the greatest of nature's displays. Among these, it is the original groves and stands containing the oldest and largest, "old growth," trees that conservationists have fought to put under public protection. The geographical definitions of these original forests have caused much debate with private and commercial interests over the years.

How to Get There

Redwood National Park, in the northeastern corner of California, extends as a narrow strip from Crescent City in the north toward Arcata in the south. San Francisco, about 330 miles south, is the nearest metropolitan area. The automobile trip from there takes less than 7 hours on a good freeway, U.S. 101.

BY CAR: The park is reached by U.S. 101 from the north and south; U.S. 199 also approaches it from the north. State 1, along the coast, is a spectacularly scenic, but much slower moving, alternate to U.S. 101 from the south.

BY BUS, RAIL, AND AIR: Contact your commercial carrier directly for their services to this area. Towns nearest the park are Orick, Klamath, and Crescent City. You can probably make connections to Arcata, about 30 miles south of the park, which has the nearest commercial airport and car rentals.

Where to Stay

Crescent City, the temporary headquarters for the national park, is the major center of tourist accommodations in this region. Nearby accommodations can also be found in the towns of Klamath and Orick, just outside of the park.

TALLEST KNOWN TREES *in the world occupy the inside of the bend of Redwood Creek.*

REDWOOD NATIONAL PARK *nature trails take you through dense stands of the ageless giant trees and growths of Western sword ferns higher than your head. This is across stream from Prairie Creek camp.*

The three state parks within Redwood National Park offer good campgrounds.

TRAVELING IN THE REDWOOD COUNTRY

If you are on your way to Redwood National Park, you are naturally most interested in seeing the ancient, towering redwoods. Your route from the south is the scenic northern California coast country, part of which you will travel on the beautiful Redwood Highway, a section of U.S. 101. Below Eureka the old highway, The Avenue of the Giants, has been retained as a turnoff from the freeway, so travelers can enjoy the redwoods while moving at a leisurely pace. Motorists traveling from the south will drive through many miles of redwood trees, including some in state parks and reserves, before they actually reach the national park.

In this area, in addition to the redwoods, there are groves of oak, spruce, alder, Douglas-fir, and madrone. Other plant life includes many varieties of ferns and hundreds of flowers and shrubs. Animal life is also abundant here.

California has 32 state parks which preserve redwood trees. Three of these make up the heart of the new Redwood National Park. They are Prairie Creek Redwoods, Del Norte Coast Redwoods, and Jedediah Smith Redwoods state parks. Though the administration of the national park itself is still in the planning stages, these three state parks offer miles of inspiring walks under the towering giants, fish-filled streams, herds of elk, wild beaches, and many fine campsites.

Prairie Creek Redwoods State Park

Just north of Orick at the southern boundary of the national park lies Prairie Creek Redwoods State Park.

WIND TRAINED *forest clings to steep Gold Bluffs; on road's other side, windy sea stretches to infinity.*

This park has 8 miles of shoreline, including historical Gold Bluffs Beach, a wide and wild beach offering an exhilarating walk along picturesque bluffs that are crowned with trees and cleaved by fern canyons. The beach got its name from the many amateur miners who panned it extensively in the 1850's. The sand still contains gold flakes, although their recovery would be unprofitable today.

You can gather driftwood along the shore here; but, typical of the northern California coast, the undertow is too dangerous for swimming.

Other attractions at the park are the sheer, fern-covered walls of Fern Canyon at the mouth of Home Creek and two herds of magnificent Roosevelt elk. You will find one herd roaming along the beach and the other in the prairie. The loop road which turns off from U.S. 101 about 2 miles north of Orick will take you to beautiful Fern Canyon, Gold Bluffs Beach, and Beach Campground.

There are 40 miles of hiking trails in the park, all beginning at park headquarters. They take you through groves of redwoods and other trees and through profuse and colorful stands of rhododendrons in the spring. Prairie Creek has trout fishing.

CLIFFS OF NORTH COAST *are constantly beat by the tide. This is Trinidad Beach south of the national park.*

FERN-COVERED WALLS *of Fern Canyon on Home Creek enclose you. This is a few yards from the beach.*

There are over a hundred campsites here, some in the prairie and some on Gold Bluffs Beach.

Big, Stone, and Freshwater lagoons, just south of the park, will accommodate boating, limited water skiing, and swimming. Freshwater Lagoon is also well known for its trout fishing.

On Redwood Creek, about 4 miles southeast of the state park, is what is known as the Emerald Mile, where the world's tallest trees were recently measured by the National Geographic Society.

Del Norte Coast Redwoods State Park

Between Klamath and Crescent City is Del Norte Coast Redwoods State Park. Del Norte has the newest and best campground of all the redwood parks. Mill Creek, which runs through the camp, provides excellent wading and swimming for children.

In Del Norte you can hike on trails to beautiful groves and to the coast with its small, rocky beaches and active surf. The path to the beach is steep and challenging. There is no fishing.

Jedediah Smith Redwoods State Park

At the northernmost end of Redwood National Park are the magnificent groves of Jedediah Smith Redwoods State Park. The area was named for the mountain man explorer, who camped at nearby Crescent City and was thought to be the first to see the great redwood trees here in 1828.

Stout Grove is one of the world's most impressive stands of trees. One tree here measures 320 feet high and 21 feet in diameter. You can reach Stout Grove over a foot bridge from Camp 64 in the summer and early fall.

Also of interest in the state park is the very primitive and narrow Howland Hills Road, which follows the original stage route here. If you know where to look, you can still see parts of the old split-log road that carried travelers a century ago.

The Smith River and others provide all-year fishing, with rainbow and cutthroat trout in spring and summer, salmon in early fall, and steelhead later in fall. The Smith River also offers a long beach with several deep swimming areas. The Klamath River, about 20 miles south, provides the angler with world famous salmon and steelhead fishing.

The state park is laced generously with trails for hikers, and has more than a hundred campsites.

You can receive more information about the new Redwood National Park by writing to the superintendent in care of the present headquarters: 501 H Street, Drawer N., Crescent City, California 95531.

DIMENSIONS OF REDWOOD FOREST *with fern-covered floor overwhelm a man standing on a log.*

NATIONAL MONUMENTS
& POINT REYES
NATIONAL SEASHORE

Contrasting lands from sand to sea to stands of tall trees

DEVILS POSTPILE'S *extraordinary basaltic formation fits together like pipes of a great organ and is set in beautiful lake and forest country. Monument also preserves other interesting geologic features.*

DEATH VALLEY'S *riffled sand flows to the far horizon in waves of wind-smoothed dunes.*

POINT REYES NATIONAL SEASHORE has the white cliffs of Drake's Bay. Here, at the end of a trail, a stream has cut its way through. The offshore "stacks" or islands are carved by winds and waves.

DEATH VALLEY

Legendary Death Valley is distinguished from other desert valleys by great size and low altitude, diversity of desert scene, and a colorful history.

Throughout the valley you'll see the marks left by human as well as geologic history. Indian petroglyphs are found in more than 200 sites. Many places carry names of pioneers and prospectors of the gold rush days. Death Valley itself was named by the first groups of pioneers crossing in 1849. Though their hardships were extreme, the fact is that only one forty-niner died during this trek through the desert. Ghosts of boom towns and mines, herds of wild burros, and the folklore of the valley echo lively days and colorful characters of the gold rush.

Death Valley National Monument was established in 1933 with 3,000 square miles of varied desert features that can be explored on over 500 miles of improved roadways. Additional miles of primitive roads wind through the back country, leading down narrow, twisting canyons or up into isolated mountain flats.

How to Get There

Death Valley National Monument is in southeastern California, with its northeast corner extending into Nevada.

BY CAR: The most spectacular and developed approach is from the west over State Highway 190 from Lone Pine to Towne's Pass. Death Valley may be reached from any direction on scenic and well kept roads.

BY BUS, RAIL, AND AIR: The Las Vegas-Tonopah-Reno Stage Line operates from Las Vegas; Riddle Scenic Tours and Tanner-Gray Line Motor Tours from Los Angeles. Check your travel agent for tours that may originate in your area.

Las Vegas, Nevada is the closest rail and air terminal to Death Valley. A paved landing strip for light planes is in the monument at Furnace Creek.

Where to Stay

Accommodations range from luxury lodges to campsites, some open all year. Normal season is October 15 through May 15, when the weather is not extremely hot.

The most luxurious place to stay is at Furnace Creek Inn with swimming pool, tennis courts, cocktail lounge, palm gardens, stables, and an 18-hole golf course. Rates are around $36.00 to $48.00 per day for two, American Plan. A mile down the road, the Furnace Creek Ranch adjoins a date-palm grove, and has a swimming pool, cocktail lounge, golf and riding facilities. Rates start about $11.00 for two, without meals. There is also a trailer court here. In the winter Furnace Creek stables offers interesting guided trips.

Stove Pipe Wells Hotel, about 30 miles north, is an informal place open all year. For diversion you'll find a swimming pool, cocktail lounge, and evening entertainment. Main season rates begin at around $14.50 for two, European Plan.

Surrounded by wooded canyon scenery, the small and rustic Wildrose Station is just inside the boundary on the road from Trona. A curio shop here has rare Indian pottery and desert glass. Cabins at this high and cool elevation are available all year and cost from $6.50 for double occupancy. Write Box 397, Trona, California 93562 for reservations.

For reservations at Furnace Creek and Stove Pipe Wells, write Death Valley, California 92328.

CAMPGROUNDS provide scenic backdrops from whispering sand dunes to sweeping mountain views. Of 11 monument campgrounds, the 3 developed ones are in the valley: Texas Spring near the visitor center;

MULEBACK TRIPS *into Furnace Creek's nearby canyons are a popular pastime of Death Valley visitors.*

THE JUMBLED MOUNTAINS *of Death Valley, striped with fantastic reds and browns, yellows and greens, take on a lunar look under glowering sky, and add to variety of terrain in the national monument.*

Furnace Creek open all year, but very hot in the summer; and Mesquite Spring south of Scotty's Castle. Secondary ones are Sand Dunes (no water) and Midway Well, both in the Stove Pipe Wells vicinity; and year-around Emigrant Junction, where you have good mountain and valley views. Campgrounds at higher elevations are open in summer.

At all camps you furnish your own trash containers and firewood; at some, the water must be boiled.

NATURAL FEATURES

Fossils of prehistoric mammals discovered in Death Valley show that these arid salt flats, gravel desert, and harsh peaks were at one time a fertile plain. In fact all of the great divisions of geologic time and nearly all of the periods that subdivide them are represented in the land formations of Death Valley.

With increasingly dry climate, ancient lakes evaporated into salt flat deposits such as Devil's Golf Course and mud playas like the Racetrack.

Wind reduced granite into sand and blew it into dunes. As the wind blows from all directions, the dunes remain trapped in place.

Death Valley is a great educational museum of geology and biology. Yet its intricate story is not over; it is still in the slow but steady hands of the earth's forces.

Plants and Animals

The popular belief that nothing lives or grows in Death Valley is discounted by the common animal and plant life. Plants have strangely adapted to their environment and can keep alive through the burning heat and dryness of summer. Almost all have deep or far-spreading roots and special adaptations of leaves and stems to help tap and conserve vital water. Over 600 species of plants and trees flourish at all elevations in the monument, and 22 species—like the Panamint daisy, Death Valley sage, rattleweed—exist only here. Bristlecone pines, thousands of years old, grow above 10,000 feet elevation on Telescope Peak.

The name Death Valley is a misnomer on a favorable spring day when the unexpected brilliance of myriads of springtime wildflowers mantle the dark alluvial slopes and narrow canyon washes.

Casual visitors to Death Valley see few animals as most are nocturnal, feeding when it is cooler. There is great variety of natural life in a 2-mile area between Telescope Peak and Badwater, where animals adapted to desert conditions get much of the moisture they need from their food. Only the plantless central salt flats are barren of animal life.

Several kinds of reptiles, small ground animals, and more than 230 kinds of birds populate Death Valley. The most commonly seen rodent is the antelope ground squirrel. In the evenings you may see kit fox, coyotes, and bobcats along the roads. It is rare to see a desert bighorn sheep, native to the rocky slopes and gorges; but you may hear serenades of the wild burros descended from the prospectors' animals from your Wildrose mountain camp. Even fish live in this desert. Descendent of Ice Age ancestors, the pupfish or "desert sardine" thrives in Salt Creek, Saratoga Springs, and Devil's Hole.

EXPLORING THE VALLEY

The forbidding name of Death Valley never rings true after you spend a day here. This is a land of light, color, and awesome beauty. Each season of the year, each hour of the day, it changes character with the shifting of light and shadow. And the long distant views cast spells with their variations in color, form, and texture.

The summer visitor may remember the blazing sun and intense heat, but at other seasons Death Valley basks in a mild climate that has made it a popular resort area. Facilities are in full operation November through mid-April. During summer a list of Hot Weather Hints, distributed in the monument, will help make your visit safe and pleasant.

The all year visitor center at Furnace Creek is the best place to begin. Museum exhibits of history, geology, flora and fauna; hourly ranger lectures in the auditorium; and brochures and maps will enhance your enjoyment of Death Valley.

Because of an excellent and dependable water supply from nearby springs, Furnace Creek has always been a center of activity. The Borax Museum at the Ranch is in what is possibly the valley's first frame house, moved from its original site in Twenty-Mule-Team Canyon where it had been a boarding house for miners.

For adventures in exploring off the main track, inquire about road information for four-wheel-drive vehicles that will take you into the rough back country. These roads are closed in summer.

THE GHOSTTOWN OF RHYOLITE, NEVADA is on State 58 just outside of the monument. Here a $130,000 railroad station without a railroad now houses a museum and store. The Rhyolite Bottle House, with walls built of 51,000 beer bottles set in adobe, is still occupied by a Rhyolite citizen selling desert glass and curios. Rhyolite, a spirited boom town around the turn of the century, lasted only five years. A rich gold strike in nearby Bullfrog Hills was responsible for the 7,000 population, elaborate buildings, and mine shafts. On a dirt road about a mile south of town lies the aging Bullfrog-Rhyolite graveyard, where you can still read some of the weathered wooden markers.

TITUS CANYON is reached by a one-way dirt road that must be entered from State 58 on the east. This 25-mile trip through the wineglass-shaped canyon with changing colors and soaring walls is exciting and beautiful. You pass the remains of short-lived Leadfield; and near Klare Spring are Indian petroglyphs. Early morning when the sun is at your back is the best time to make this trip. Check road conditions before you go.

SCOTTY'S CASTLE is the fantastic desert mansion of Death Valley Scotty (Walter Scott) and his millionaire friend A. M. Johnson. In the extreme northern part of the monument, the Spanish-Moorish mansion lavishly furnished took about 10 years to build and cost 2 million dollars. Scotty's flamboyant escapades became part of Death Valley folklore, and the castle remains as a testimony to his natural showmanship and eccentric personality. Hourly tours daily from 9 A.M. to 6 P.M. have an admission charge. Gift shop and snack bar are open for visitors.

COLORFUL UBEHEBE CRATER, one-half mile wide and 800 feet deep, was caused about 3,000 years ago by a volcanic explosion, and is a short drive from Scotty's Castle.

THE RACETRACK, 27 miles south of the crater, is a mud playa, occasionally subject to high velocity winds that are believed to cause the "mystery of the moving rocks."

HARMONY BORAX WORKS' extensive ruins are on State 190 north of Furnace Creek. A 2-mile, sometimes muddy walk northwest across the salt flats takes you to mounds of dried mud looking like haystacks, which once yielded a form of borax. North of the refinery, a 1-mile dirt road leads to Mustard Canyon, colored by oxidizing iron.

ZABRISKIE POINT, southeast of Furnace Creek on the same road, is an area of ancient lake beds, 5 to 10 million years old, that is especially dramatic and colorful at sunrise.

DANTE'S VIEW, on the crest of the Black Mountains, is one of the most spectacular scenic overlooks in America. It is a point 5,755 feet in elevation directly above Badwater, which is 282 feet below sea level.

ARTIST'S DRIVE, off the main road south of Furnace Creek, takes you through a rainbow canyon colored by oxidation. The even more intense color of Artist's Pallette is splashed on a hillside halfway through.

BADWATER, a few miles farther south, is known as the lowest point in the western hemisphere (−282 feet). The salt pools are often crusted over, and close up reveal fantastic formations of rugged rock salt.

Superintendent of Death Valley National Monument: Death Valley, California 92328.

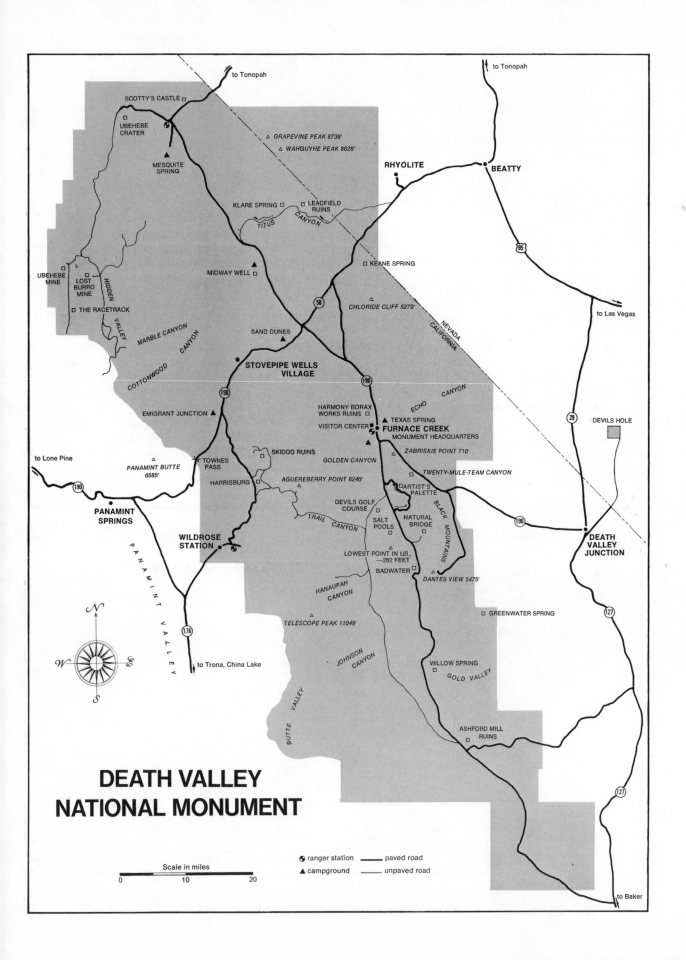

to Tonopah

to Tonopah

SCOTTY'S CASTLE

UBEHEBE CRATER

MESQUITE SPRING

△ GRAPEVINE PEAK 8738'

△ WAHGUYHE PEAK 8628'

RHYOLITE

BEATTY

KLARE SPRING

LEADFIELD RUINS

TITUS

CANYON

KEANE SPRING

95

UBEHEBE MINE

LOST BURRO MINE

HIDDEN VALLEY

THE RACETRACK

MIDWAY WELL

58

△ CHLORIDE CLIFF 5279'

to Las Vegas

NEVADA

CALIFORNIA

MARBLE CANYON

CANYON

SAND DUNES

COTTONWOOD

CANYON

STOVEPIPE WELLS VILLAGE

190

29

DEVILS HOLE

190

EMIGRANT JUNCTION ▲

ECHO

CANYON

HARMONY BORAX WORKS RUINS

▲ TEXAS SPRING

VISITOR CENTER

FURNACE CREEK

MONUMENT HEADQUARTERS

to Lone Pine

△ PANAMINT BUTTE 6585'

TOWNES PASS

SKIDOO RUINS

GOLDEN CANYON

ZABRISKIE POINT 710'

TWENTY-MULE-TEAM CANYON

190

HARRISBURG

AGUEREBERRY POINT 6240'

ARTIST'S PALETTE

DEVILS GOLF COURSE

BLACK

DEATH VALLEY JUNCTION

190

PANAMINT SPRINGS

PANAMINT VALLEY

WILDROSE STATION

TRAIL CANYON

SALT POOLS

NATURAL BRIDGE

MOUNTAINS

LOWEST POINT IN U.S., —282 FEET

BADWATER

DANTES VIEW 5475'

178

HANAUPAH CANYON

GREENWATER SPRING

127

△ TELESCOPE PEAK 11049'

to Trona, China Lake

JOHNSON CANYON

WILLOW SPRING

GOLD VALLEY

BUTTE VALLEY

ASHFORD MILL RUINS

DEATH VALLEY NATIONAL MONUMENT

N

W E

S

127

Scale in miles

0   10   20

⊕ ranger station   —— paved road

▲ campground   — unpaved road

to Baker

JOSHUA TREE

Located in the beautiful high desert country of Southern California, Joshua Tree is a national monument primarily because of the great diversity and richness of its desert vegetation. On the border between the Mojave and Colorado deserts, it preserves another transition country and vast desert region with distinctive plants and animals that have adapted to the extreme heat and aridity of their environment.

The Joshua-tree itself is a large yucca (Y. brevifolia), one of the most spectacular plants of the southwestern deserts. It has been known to grow to 40 feet tall, and has clusters of white blossoms to 14 inches long at the ends of its angular branches. Growing at 3,000 to 5,000 feet elevation in the central and western portions of the monument, the Joshua-tree, a member of the lily family, will bloom in March and April, except during exceptionally dry years when there will be no blossoms. It is believed the Mormons named the "Joshua Tree" or "praying plant" because of its upstretching arms. The plant is often confused with the Mohave yucca, which is more common at lower elevations and is distinguished by much longer leaves.

In addition to extensive stands of Joshua-trees, the monument has many kinds of cactus with large showy blossoms, the spidery ocotillo, and the feathery plumed nolina. The stately Washingtonia palm is found growing in several of the shady oases. One grove in Lost Palm Canyon contains more than one hundred.

As in Death Valley, the spring wildflower show at Joshua Tree National Monument is dependent upon winter rains. Average annual rainfall here is 5 inches, and in a normal year the color show begins at lower elevations as early as March and progresses to higher altitudes through June.

Wildlife in the monument resembles that in Death Valley and similar desert regions, but it is more abundant because of higher altitudes, cooler and more varied climate. As with the plant life, adaptation is necessary to the animal's survival. The kangaroo rat with his long tufted tail is often seen around campgrounds at night. This adaptable creature and some other rodents manufacture water in their own bodies and can go a lifetime without a drink. The largest animal, the desert bighorn sheep, is impressive, but rarely seen. You're most likely to observe the lively side-blotched lizard (little brown uta). There have been 249 kinds of birds reported in Joshua Tree (many of them migrants) and 38 species of reptiles and amphibians.

History of human habitation is written throughout the monument. Discoveries of ancient artifacts along an

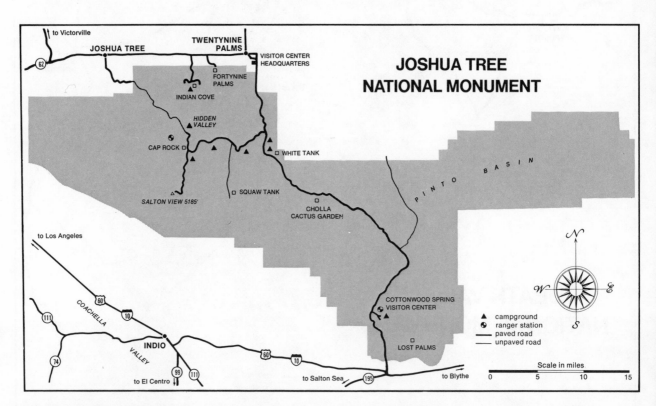

JOSHUA TREE NATIONAL MONUMENT, like Death Valley, preserves a choice parcel of the steadily diminishing Southern California desert, including its varied and abundant plant and animal life.

THE JOSHUA-TREE or "praying plant," named by Mormons for its upstretched arms, can grow to 40 feet.

WONDERLAND OF ROCKS in Hidden Valley was understandably known as a rustler and badman hideout.

ancient river terrace in the Pinto Basin indicate the presence of primitive man in the days when there was water to support a culture. Much later Indians who mastered the art of survival in the desert settled at springs and waterholes, and left traces of their campsites. The first white men in the area were gold prospectors around 1865. Their mark remains as old mine shafts and mills on the hillsides; and the cattlemen who followed left small dams, or "tanks," to catch rainwater for their herds.

Your trip to Joshua Tree can be full of beautiful and interesting stops. An early visit to the visitor center and museum at monument headquarters near Twentynine Palms will acquaint you with the fascinating land you are about to explore. A small visitor center is near the south entrance in the Cottonwood Spring area, a palm oasis noted for its bird life.

Hidden Valley's massive boulders and interesting rock formations are a legendary rustlers' hideout. The Wonderland of Rocks now shelters a campground and is a good place for rock scrambling.

Salton View will give you a sweeping view of a fine desert scene. From 5,185 feet, you have a panorama ranging from 235 feet below sea level at the Salton Sea to over 10,000 feet at San Jacinto Peak and San Gorgonio Mountain, highest in Southern California. This view includes the Coachella Valley with its famous date gardens.

You'll find other attractions along your way, including Cap Rock, Lost Horse Valley, Indian Cove, Pinto Basin, the oases with their shady palm trees, and Cholla Cactus Garden which has a self-guiding nature trail. All contribute to an enjoyable desert experience.

Planning a Visit

The monument is an area of 872 square miles located 150 miles east of Los Angeles. From the west, it is approached on U.S. Highway 60 (Interstate 10) to a point 15 miles east of Banning, then north on State 62 to the towns of Joshua Tree and Twentynine Palms and the north entrance. From the north and U.S. 66, turn south at Amboy 50 miles to Twentynine Palms. The south, Cottonwood Spring, entrance is 25 miles east of Indio, on U.S. 60 (I-10). Main roads inside the monument are surfaced and suitable for trailers, if taken cautiously. Visitors should carry water in the summer.

The monument is open all year, but its main season is October 15 to May 15.

There are no lodging or eating facilities within the monument, but accommodations are found in and near the entrance towns.

There are several good campgrounds inside the monument, but you will have to furnish fuel and water. Cottonwood Campground near the south entrance does have running water. Otherwise, there are water pickup stations between Ryan and Sheep Pass campgrounds, and at the visitor center in Twentynine Palms.

Superintendent of Joshua Tree National Monument: Box 875, Twentynine Palms, California 92277.

PINNACLES

Rocky spires and crags, the pinnacles, rise abruptly against the sky to 1,200 feet above the various canyon floors. These last remnants of an ancient volcano tell the geologic story of this land that contrasts sharply with the smooth rounded country that surrounds it. The pinnacles, several caves, and many good hiking trails open this national monument to the interest of visitors. Fall through spring are the favorite visitor months, as the heat of the summer discourages some.

Chaparral dominates the plant life in this area. The wildlife you can expect to see include the blacktailed deer; the gray fox and bobcat are common but more nocturnal. Bats come out at night for insects.

For adventure, you should see the Old Pinnacles area on the west side of the park. From the end of the road you walk into a narrow defile between the spectacular overhangs of Machete Ridge and The Balconies. You will need a flashlight. Huge boulders, wedged into the gorge, interrupt the natural skylights. The caves do not have maintained trails, so be careful not to get disoriented. You will crawl, stretch, duck, and squeeze along for a few hundred feet clear through the caves, and come out into daylight on the other side. Children should not go into the caves alone. With a light there is little danger in the caves, but slippery places, low "ceilings," and drop-offs are hazards in the dark.

Hiking is very popular at Pinnacles, as most of the trails form loops and are not too long. Some short and easy trips are in the caves area around Bear Gulch, where the visitor center and a picnic area are located, and from the end of the paved road on the east side to meet the road on the west. More strenuous trips are the High Peaks Trail, opening up beautiful views of the surrounding country, and the trail to North Chalone Peak, where you'll find a fire lookout. Varied trails pass through cool shady nooks with ferns onto hot, dry slopes.

The monument entrance and most of the facilities are on the east side, reached via Hollister or King City (both 35 miles away) on State Highway 25. State 146 from Soledad enters the park from the west and ends a short way inside the boundary at a walk-in campground. The monument has no east-west connecting road.

The monument has campgrounds and picnic areas. Bring your own fuel. Nearest supplies are at Paicines.

Superintendent of Pinnacles National Monument: Paicines, California 95043.

SPECTACULAR PINNACLES and spires, remnants of an ancient volcano, contrast with surrounding country.

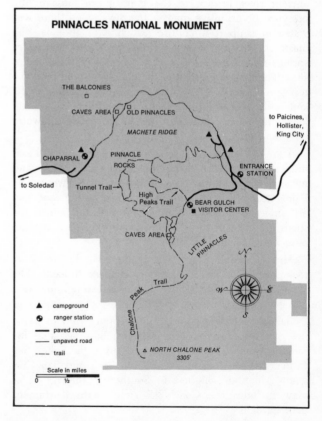

PINNACLES NATIONAL MONUMENT, enjoyable any season, has hiking trails to caves, canyons, views.

DEVILS POSTPILE

In the midst of beautiful forest and lake country west of Mammoth Lakes and a few miles southeast of Yosemite, a geological oddity is on permanent display in Devils Postpile National Monument.

Symmetrical basaltic columns, some rising more than 60 feet and fitting together to resemble a great pipe organ, are remnants of a lava flow at least 915,000 years ago which cracked into columns as it cooled. The Middle Fork glacier 200,000 years ago quarried away much of this mass of basalt. Of the resistant formations left standing, Devils Postpile is the largest, 900 feet long and 200 feet high. Most of the columns are vertical, but some are slanting, some are curved, and others seem to radiate out from a common center. You can walk up the unexposed side and stand on a beautifully smoothed mosaic floor where the action of the ice overran and polished the tops of the columns.

The Devils Postpile is one of the key features of the John Muir Trail that runs between Yosemite and Sequoia national parks.

Of geological interest too is the pumice found in the northern part of the monument. This porous volcanic rock, so light that it floats in water, was deposited by volcanoes east and north of the Postpile. Recent volcanic activity is also hinted at by several bubbling hot springs, including one at Reds Meadow.

The Middle Fork of the San Joaquin River, flowing through the monument, offers fairly good fishing. Two miles down the river trail from the Postpile, you will see it become the beautiful Rainbow Fall dropping 140 feet over the dark basaltic cliffs into a pool. Watch your footing on the unstable pumice stone when watching the fall from the edge of the gorge. You can take the steep trail to the bottom of the fall into a lovely garden.

Devils Postpile is open from about June 15 to October 1. The monument is a long narrow area entered from the northeast via an 18-mile road from U.S. 395.

A campground is also open mid-June to October depending on the weather. Just south of it is a spring of soda water. Try it straight or mix it with lemon juice and sugar. There are no accommodations within the monument, but 2 miles from the campground, Reds Meadow has cabins, meals, supplies, and saddle and pack horses.

Superintendent of Devils Postpile National Monument: Yosemite National Park, California 95389.

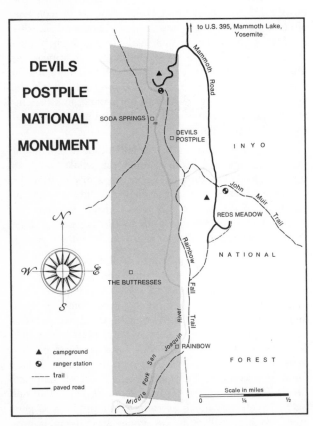

DEVILS POSTPILE NATIONAL MONUMENT lies in the magnificent forest and lake country near Yosemite.

SYMMETRICAL BASALTIC COLUMNS are central feature of monument and a key point on John Muir Trail.

CABRILLO

ACRES OF TIDE POOLS can be studied at low tide; at high tide, water reaches cliffs below Point Loma light.

The discovery of the California coast is commemorated by beautiful Cabrillo National Monument, about 10 miles from downtown San Diego. In 1542, Portuguese explorer Juan Rodríguez Cabrillo left Mexico in the service of Spain and became the first explorer to visit the shores of what is today California and Oregon. Ballast Point, where the actual landing was made in this area, is not part of the monument; but it is easily seen from a nearby cliff-top overlook that also has an open view well into Mexico. On Point Loma overlooking the bay, Cabrillo National Monument is popular for outstanding seascapes and a picturesque old lighthouse. A statue of Cabrillo (his Hispanicized name), which was a gift from Portugal, has also become a familiar feature of the monument.

The visitor center has an exhibit room depicting Cabrillo's historic voyage and an auditorium for programs about the monument. Nearby, from a glass-enclosed building you have a spectacular view of the harbor and the city of San Diego.

The old lighthouse, built in 1854, was one of the eight government authorized lighthouses for the West coast and operated for about 40 years. As the lighthouse thrusts 462 feet above San Diego Bay, its beacon was often obscured by fog, and it was abandoned in 1891 for another light station that could be more easily seen at sea. Inside the old 1854 lighthouse, it appears as though the last light keeper, who served there for 20 years, had just stepped out for a moment. Climb the lighthouse tower any clear day for a panorama that includes the Coronado Islands and mountains far beyond the mesa of La Jolla.

But there is more at this small national monument than panorama and history. From the whale watching station, December through February, you can spot the telltale 15-foot spouts of the California gray whale, as hundreds of the gray giants pass Cabrillo on their migration from the Arctic Ocean to the lagoons of Baja California to mate and then return to bear their young.

You can also walk a nature trail for half an hour below the whale watching station and part way down the headland's west slope, to see a coastal plant community that braves the salt-laden winds. Some surprises include rare cactus that grow only on the coast. A little-known aspect of Point Loma is some of the best tide pools left in Southern California with fascinating creatures of the sea in an area preserved in its natural state for over a century. They are reached just off Gatchell Road. The broad flats the tide uncovers here have not been depleted as much as some other public tide pool areas, because collecting specimens from them is prohibited. Tide pool exploring is at its best from about 3 hours minus tide to 3 hours after. Newspapers list the tide's exact times each day. Wear sneakers, so you can wade in the pools without cutting your feet, and replace rocks you lift for inspection, so you don't disturb the creatures' habitat. You'll probably see such marine life as starfish, sea anemone, crabs, sea hares, or even baby octopus.

You can reach Point Loma easily by driving southwest from San Diego on Rosecrans Street or from Mission Bay on Sunset Cliffs Boulevard to Catalina Boulevard. The monument is open daily, 9 A.M. to 5:30 P.M., except June 18 through Labor Day, when it is open until 8 P.M. To arrive at Point Loma, you must pass through U.S. Navy property. There are no camping or eating facilities inside the Navy gates.

Superintendent of Cabrillo National Monument: Box 6175, San Diego, California 92106.

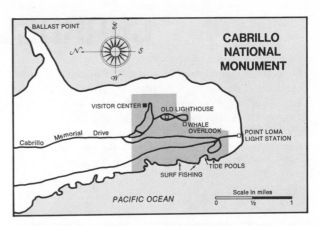

CABRILLO NATIONAL MONUMENT covers a very small area at the tip of Point Loma on San Diego Bay.

CABRILLO STATUE, gift of Portugal, celebrates history, the first exploration of the California coast.

FROM 1855 TO 1891, navigators approaching San Diego relied on lamp in tower of old Point Loma lighthouse.

CHANNEL ISLANDS

The eight Channel Islands extend in a northwesterly direction off the coast of Southern California from San Diego to Point Conception, about 10 to 70 miles offshore. In 1938, the two smallest islands, Anacapa and Santa Barbara, which are 40 miles apart, were set aside as a national monument to protect the rare plant and animal life of these wild and beautiful preserves.

Once part of the mainland, the islands are really small mountain tops reaching above the Pacific Ocean.

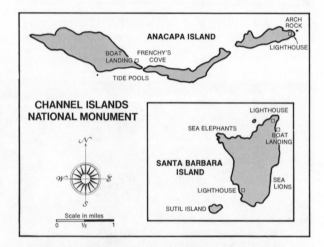

CHANNEL ISLANDS *National Monument is actually two of a group of offshore islands near Los Angeles.*

LANDMARK ARCH *just east of Anacapa frames the schooner-rigged clipper* Swift of Ipswich.

The northern four, including Anacapa, are part of the seaward-going Santa Monica Mountains that begin in Los Angeles. As a result of this separation, 80 plants and several animals have evolved into subspecies or species different from their mainland relatives, and are found nowhere else in the world. Here, the scientist and nature lover has the chance to observe and enjoy the effects of geographical isolation.

If the two islands have a trademark, it could be the striking endemic plant, the giant coreopsis (*Coreopsis gigantea*). Often reaching 6 to 8 feet in height, the curious perennial dominates the spring wildflower display on the islands with brilliant splashes of yellow seen from far out at sea.

ANACAPA ISLAND, only about 10 miles off the coast of Port Hueneme, is really a narrow rocky chain of three islands about 5 miles long. As you approach, Anacapa looks romantic with the distant charm of any landfall, then austere for lack of trees, then fascinating when you can make out clearly its caves, coves, and cliffs.

The landing place on the north side is a bight just west of the break between the middle and western islands. This is Frenchy's Cove, site of a temporary park ranger station manned during the summer season. A few level spots afford space for Spartan camping. Here you can swim, look into a small cave, climb a precipitous path to the razor-edge spine of the island, cross to walk along the south shore beach, and, at low tide, explore some superlative tide pools.

Sailing east along the north shore, you can see Anacapa's most prominent grove of trees, blue gum eucalyptus, high in a draw on the western third of the middle island. If you trace the draw down to the shore you will see a tiny inlet in the rock where a skilled boatman can put people ashore. A path on the inlet's left side will take you exploring.

The east island has few landings, but it does have a spectacular cave, navigable by dinghy in calm water through its northwesterly point.

The south side has two anchorages, in the East Fish Camp and Cat Rock areas. The south coast cliffs look steeper, rawer, more recently eroded. Here, where it is sunnier, you will see the most sea lions, dozing in little coves or frolicking in the water.

The sea cliffs on both islands provide nesting areas for many sea birds. There are more favorable areas for sea mammals on Santa Barbara Island than on Anacapa.

SANTA BARBARA ISLAND is 38 miles opposite San Pedro, the port of Los Angeles. Almost vertical sea cliffs up to 500 feet high back small rocky bays and sandy beaches that attract marine mammals, including the California sea lions that are a great attraction of the

SANDY BEACH AND TIDE POOLS on the south shore of Anacapa's west island are uncovered by low tide, and visitors can picnic and explore the fascinating area. Offshore stack is Cat Rock.

monument. Dramatic seascapes are the rule at Santa Barbara Island with its several caves, offshore pillars, and blowholes that spout spray. The 50 to 60-degree ocean temperature surrounding the island contributes to its year-around moderate climate.

Skin and SCUBA diving off both islands is best in the winter. Anchorage at Santa Barbara Island is usually confined to the sheltered area on the northeast side.

Planning a Visit

The undeveloped islands have no accommodations, no fresh water, and no pier facilities. To go ashore you should have a skiff or other small boat. Mariners should have the *Coast Pilot*, published by the Navy Hydrographic Office, and navigational charts (U.S. Coast and Geodetic Survey charts 5110 and 5114) for island details. Sightseeing charter vessels and fishing party boats out of Channel Island Harbor, Ventura Marina, and

Port Hueneme can be engaged for the trip. Also marina operators may direct you to available private boats.

During the wildflower blooming season between April and mid-June, the Sierra Club takes a boating party out of the city of Santa Barbara aboard the sleek *Swift of Ipswich*, a Baltimore clipper topsail schooner with a diesel engine, that lands in Anacapa and circles the other islands. They also take overnight trips to Anacapa. Minimum age for the cruises is 10 years; children between 10 and 15 must be accompanied by an adult. For information, write Mrs. Kenneth R. Fortney, 429 E. Figueroa #9, Santa Barbara, California 93101.

Both islands permit camping, but remember that nights are windy and cool, and that you must supply your own food, water, and fuel.

A National Park Service boat patrols Anacapa and Santa Barbara islands the year around.

Superintendent of Channel Islands National Monument: Box 1388, Oxnard, California 93030.

LAVA BEDS

The rugged and fascinating landscape of Lava Beds National Monument in Northern California was formed by volcanic activity, ancient and recent. Its most conspicuous features are the smooth cinder cones rising to 500 feet above the lava beds. Among the largest of these cones is Schonchin Butte, named after a famous war chief of the Modoc Indians. Most of the 17 cinder cones are in the southern part of the monument.

Chimney-like formations, like Fleener Chimneys northwest of headquarters, and the unique lava tubes are other noticeable and distinctive features of the monument.

Nearly 300 lava tubes, or caves, have been found in the monument. The greatest concentration is along the Cave Loop Road near monument headquarters. Other caves, including several ice caves, are accessible from the main road. Twenty of them are open for exploration. The caves were formed when frothy, pahoehoe-type lava flowed from deep volcanic cracks in the earth's crust. The surface hardened on exposure to the air, but the hot lava beneath the crust continued to flow, forming cavelike lava tubes. When the flow in the tubes diminished, lava-stalactites formed by the cooling of the liquid lava splashed against the ceilings.

Water drains into the lower levels of some of the caves and freezes each winter. The ice remains the year around in a few, because the warm summer air does not displace the heavier cold air at the lower levels. At Merrill Ice Cave you can see a frozen waterfall and a perennial river of ice.

A contrast is Fern Cave where a floor of ferns and mosses gives the appearance of a lush garden in rugged surroundings. There are also Indian pictographs on the walls of the cave.

Gasoline lanterns for exploring the caves are available at monument headquarters. You guide yourself on tours of the caves, where trails are well defined and your descent is eased by wooden staircases.

Above-ground trails, which are short and easy hikes, include one to the top of Schonchin Butte with exceptional views of the area.

Lava Beds is also prominent for its history. The

LAVA FLOW REMNANTS and rugged terrain contrast with the growing things in Lava Beds.

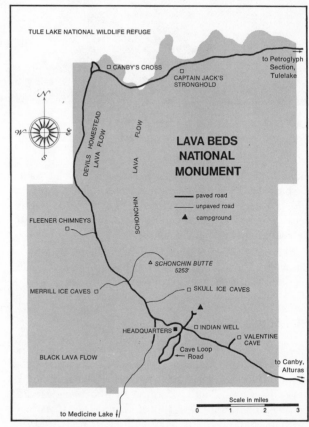

LAVA BEDS NATIONAL MONUMENT is natural, historical preserve between Crater Lake and Lassen parks.

Petroglyph Section of the monument on one of the ancient volcano cones testifies to the activities of prehistoric Indians in this area. The trail to Big Painted Cave and Symbol Bridge leads to some of these ancient markings. A lava fortress and tales of battle relate the tragic and more recent history of the last stand of the Modoc Indians against invading civilization, the only major Indian war fought in California. This war is said to be one of the country's costliest, considering the number of adversary engaged. Some 500 troops fought for several months in 1872-73 against never more than 71 Modoc warriors commanded by Captain Jack. Canby's Cross and Captain Jack's Stronghold, the almost impregnable natural fortress in the lava, are among the many historic sites of the war in the northern section of the monument.

Geologically and historically important, this 72-square-mile area was established as a national monument in 1925.

The northeast section of the monument is detached from the main area. This is the Petroglyph Section, where Indian writings are carved on the bluffs of Tule Lake. At the lake too, the wildlife refuge attracts throngs of ducks, geese, and other birds during spring and fall migrations.

Unexpectedly in this strange land, the plant life is extremely colorful. In spring and summer, spectacular colors from among the 250 species of plants spring up in contrast to the dry, black lava flows. There are about 50 species of mammals here. In late fall and winter the mule deer will come from the high country to feed. The Tule Lake National Wildlife Refuge, adjoining the monument on the north, protects millions of birds, particularly in spring and autumn during migrations. The Lava Beds area has about 200 species of birds.

Lava Beds is California's northernmost national monument, and is on the way from Lassen to Crater Lake National Park in Oregon. Located very close to the California-Oregon line, it is just off California Highway 139 or a few miles east of U.S. 97. Lava Beds is open all year and is relatively cool in the summer.

The Indian Well Campground is near monument headquarters in the southern section. In summer there are daily illustrated talks on geology at the headquarters, where there is also a museum, and in Mushpot Cave, and campfire programs each evening at the campground. Food, gasoline, and lodgings can be obtained at nearby towns of Tulelake and Newell on State 139.

Superintendent of Lava Beds National Monument: Box 867, Tulelake, California 96134.

LAVA-TUBE CAVES, intriguing and distinctive features of the monument, are easily reached and can be explored by lantern light. The greatest concentration of caves is along Cave Loop Road.

MUIR WOODS

Awesome stands of the aged yet ageless redwood trees towering above a heavily vegetated canyon floor are preserved as Muir Woods National Monument. The only place in the world where these beautiful trees still grow in their natural environment is in widely separated stands and groves within a narrow strip on the Pacific Coast from Monterey, California up to Oregon. Muir Woods is one of these groves, surrounded by wooded hills and grassland of the Coast Range.

Muir Woods National Monument is only 17 miles north of downtown San Francisco and attracts many tourists, especially on weekends. It is reached easily over the Golden Gate Bridge on U.S. 101 and State 1. Sightseeing buses are available to the monument from the city. Winter finds fewer visitors to the Woods, and more fog and chance of rain.

CATHEDRAL-LIKE GROVE of Redwoods in Muir Woods filters sunlight to fern-covered forest floor.

Within Muir Woods, the mood changes constantly with the shadows and the temperature as sunlight filters through different openings in the tall trees or the sea mists settle in their crowns. Ferns covering the springy canyon floor, California laurels bent into surrealistic shapes in their growth toward the light, the tiny winter wren constantly moving silently and almost unseen about the ground, and Redwood Creek quietly on its way to the ocean—all help create an engulfing calm. The short main trail follows the creek and has unobtrusive signs identifying the natural features. You can cross one of the wooden bridges for the return walk. If you want to do more exploring off the main trail, there are two trails that climb high up the canyon wall to lookouts where you have a panoramic view to either side of the Golden Gate. There is a total of 6 miles of trails within the monument, all connecting at one point or another with those of Mount Tamalpais State Park to offer a variety of hikes.

The tallest measured tree in the monument is 236 feet, located near a bridge north of Bohemian Grove. A venerable old Douglas-fir near the mouth of Fern Canyon, the donor's favorite, is dedicated to Congressman William Kent who presented all the land for Muir Woods to the federal government so it could be maintained in its primitive condition for future generations. The national monument was established in 1908. Kent's only request was that it be named for naturalist John Muir, who also worked to save the great redwoods.

The extremely shady conditions within Muir Woods discourages the plants that most animals like for food, so you will not see much large wildlife. Squirrels and raccoons live here, as do salamanders, moles, and other small animals. The blacktailed deer come into the redwoods when food is thin on the upper hillsides. In January and February, Redwood Creek is swollen with winter rains, and silver salmon and steelhead trout fight their way up rapids to spawning places in the monument. The salmon will die after spawning. Muir Woods is closed to fishing.

Muir Woods is strictly a day-use area, opening at eight in the morning and closing at sunset every day of the year including holidays. You will experience less congestion of visitors and enjoy the woods more during the early morning or late afternoon hours. Rangers will guide groups through with special arrangement. Admission is 50 cents for those 16 and over, or free with the annual Federal recreation passport.

The monument has no picnic or camp sites, but facilities can be found at Mount Tamalpais State Park and nearby camps.

Superintendent of Muir Woods National Monument: Mill Valley, California 94941.

POINT REYES NATIONAL SEASHORE

Tall white cliffs on the sea that attracted Sir Francis Drake in 1579, wind-carved offshore islands, expanse of sandy beach rolled over by ceaseless waves, lagoons and esteros enclosed by sand dunes and rolling hills, and forest-covered ridges—and inland—fresh water lakes, shifting sand dunes, grassy lowlands, and rugged canyons—this amazingly varied terrain belongs to Point Reyes, the West's first national seashore. Authorized in 1962 for 53,000 acres, Point Reyes National Seashore is located approximately 35 miles northwest of San Francisco and approached easily by U.S. 101 and Sir Francis Drake Boulevard or the scenic coast route, State 1.

Point Reyes Peninsula is truly an "island in time." It has been sliding northwestward along the San Andreas Fault for some 80 million years. Rocks that make up Point Reyes are geologically similar to those in the Tehachapi Mountains near Bakersfield, more than 300 miles to the south. In the 1906 earthquake, the whole sliver of land coast from Point Arena through Bodega Head and down to the southern tip of Point Reyes Peninsula took a sudden leap that resulted in spectacular dislocations of roads, fences, and buildings—as much as 20 feet in areas near the head of Tomales Bay. Point

Reyes is still moving up the coast at the rate of about 2 inches a year.

Flora on the peninsula indicates that this has long been a merging point of northern and southern California coast range plants. While the Douglas-fir stands are typical of those that grow much farther north, the forests of Bishop pine resemble those in the southern part of the state. Six species of plants are found nowhere else but on the peninsula, and a small grove of coast redwoods is an attraction that adds to the variety of growing things.

Because of the diversified climate, terrain, and plant life, the wildlife at Point Reyes ranges widely, from shore birds and animals to dense mountain dwellers. There are 312 species of birds and 96 species of mammals recorded here, among them the mountain beaver, a "living fossil."

The Indians and Sir Francis

For the Coast Miwok Indians the peninsula was considered the abode of the dead, but this didn't stop them from living there. Numerous mounds mark village sites,

POINT REYES PROMONTORY is in far-sweeping coast and land view from Inverness Ridge. Area is noted for variety with long beaches, sand dunes, lagoons, cliffs, forested ridges, grassland, brushy slopes.

particularly along the shores of Tomales Bay and Drake's Bay, where villagers gathered the abundant shellfish.

In 1579, Sir Francis Drake landed his ship, the *Golden Hinde,* in a place that sounds, in his chaplain's account, very much like Drake's Bay. The chaplain described "white bankes and cliffes" like those at Dover, cool, foggy weather, and moorlike land. Drake was met by the Coast Miwoks and may have given them the Ming porcelains found in village mounds.

Attractions and Activities

These are years of transition for the peninsula. About one-third of the 53,000 acres allotted to the park has been acquired from its private ownership, and the National Park Service is building up the natural history, history, and recreation potential of this unusual area. Park headquarters is near the eastern boundary at Bear Valley Ranch, 1 mile west of Olema. A trail system of nearly 60 miles now exists in the Bear Valley area, very popular with hikers, horsemen, and bike riders.

Point Reyes National Seashore is open all year, but February through April, with the lush greenness and brilliant flower displays of spring, provides the most outstanding scenery.

Fishing within the seashore proper is confined to surf fishing from open beaches, abalone diving, and clam digging. The best fishing in the area is from boats in Tomales Bay and the Pacific Ocean. Tomales Bay and Bodega Bay have launching facilities and some boat rentals. There is fresh water fishing for trout in some of the small streams and lakes in the area.

Two distinct areas are now open to the visitor. You can reach the major beaches and the dairylands through Inverness to the north, and the Bear Valley trails and hilly forest of Inverness Ridge through park headquarters.

THE BEAR VALLEY TRAILS are in the southern part of the national seashore. From park headquarters, the main trail leads 4 miles along creeks and through fir groves and meadows to the sea, where picnickers and sunbathers are welcome to use the beaches. Where the creek cuts its way through the cliffs, you'll come across tunnels and pocket beaches to explore.

For hikers, side trails lead up to the right and left along the main trail, some very steep. The trail up 1,407-foot Mount Wittenberg seems difficult looking up from the bottom, but both the walk and the view from the summit are thoroughly enjoyable. You climb through fir forest to the grassy, rounded meadows at the top of

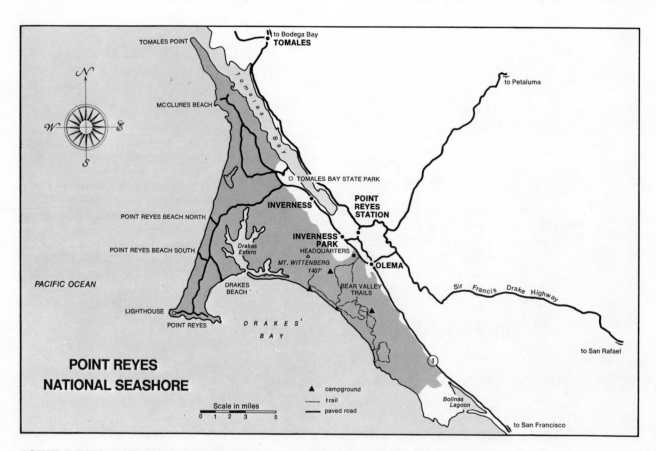

POINT REYES NATIONAL SEASHORE is on a peninsula located barely 35 miles northwest of San Francisco. Good trail system in Bear Valley adds dimension to the varied activities available here.

Wittenberg. On a clear day, you can see the entire sweep of Drake's Bay, out to distant Point Reyes. From the top you can follow the ridge trail to the sea or make a shorter loop and rejoin the main trail.

POINT REYES BEACH has two entrances about 3 miles apart. The beach remains in a wild state of crashing breakers, long stretches of sand, high grassy dunes, and sea mists. You'll find picnic tables among the dunes, drinking water, and rest rooms. Swimming and deep wading is forbidden because of the dangerous undertow and steep descent of the beach.

DRAKE'S BEACH, a fine sandy stretch backing against tall cliffs that protect it from the strong ocean winds, is good for sunning, picnicking, and swimming, also for walks west to the cliffs or east to Drake's Estero. It has a bathhouse and food service. You reach Drake's Beach by a left turn off Sir Francis Drake Boulevard.

Drake's Estero, a fingered bay that like Tomales Bay has commercial oyster beds, will be opened in the future to boating and swimming.

The lighthouse at the tip of Point Reyes is administered by the Coast Guard and not open to the public.

McCLURE'S BEACH is on a protected cove at the northern end of the Peninsula.

TOMALES BAY STATE PARK, just north of Inverness, is not part of the national seashore. It includes a fine stretch of beach on the protected bay, where sailboats move back and forth in front of the smooth mainland hills. The water gets deeper gradually and is excellent for small children.

Where to Stay

Overnight accommodations are limited in the area. Three small "pack-in" campgrounds are maintained as adjuncts to the trail system in the Bear Valley section. The closest you can drive to them is the Bear Valley Ranger Station. Fewest miles distant (3.8 miles), but the steepest climb is Sky Camp, just below the summit of Mount Wittenberg. Coast Camp is near the ocean, 8 fairly level miles away; and Glen Camp is a 5½-mile hike. A stay of one night is the limit at each camp; it is a good idea to make reservations for a site. All campers must have fire and camping permits from the Bear Valley Ranger Station.

There are motels outside the park near Inverness. The nearest campground is at Samuel P. Taylor State Park, about 6 miles east of Point Reyes headquarters.

Superintendent of Point Reyes National Seashore: Point Reyes, California 94956.

WESTWARD-RUNNING STREAM beside one Bear Valley trail tunnels under the rocks to the sea.

McCLURE'S BEACH is a small cliff-backed beach reached by a short trail from parking area.

INDEX